THE SECOND BOOK OF IRISH MYTHS
AND LEGENDS

The Second Book of Irish Myths and Legends

EOIN NEESON

THE MERCIER PRESS
4 BRIDGE STREET, CORK

© Eoin Neeson, 1966
First published 1966
Second impression 1968
Third impression 1971
SBN 85342 131 5

Contents

Introduction 7

The Children of Lir 15

Diarmuid and Graine 52

The Sickbed of Cuchulain 110

Introduction

Elsewhere the evidence – conjectural and circumstantial, nonetheless considerable – has been given[1] in support of the theory that the Irish Celts came to Ireland via the Mediterranean and that they were Ionic or Scythian (or more likely an intermingling of the two) in origin. There is a substantial basis for this argument – on the grounds that the Ionic Milesians of Miletus in Asia Minor (what is now the west coast of modern Turkey, who were a Phoenician people, searovers and colonisers with a colony in Tartessia in Spain) can be directly linked with the Irish folk tradition which maintains that the Milesians came to Ireland (about) 3,000 B.C. from Spain.

Nevertheless nowhere more than in support of – or, indeed, in opposition to – a controversial theory will 'Micawberism' more generously materialise; and something additional is always bound to turn up. The arguments in support of the theory outlined above are grouped roughly under these headings: The similarity in spirit, characterisation, structure and quality between the Graeco/Roman mythological cycles and the Celtic, as opposed to the dark and sombre background of the other European mainstream of legend, the Germanic/Scandinavian. The fact that, apart from the Graeco/Roman, the Irish literary tradition of these legends is both older by several centuries, and altogether more sophisticated, than its earliest European counterpart. The suggestion, (which cannot be proved but which scholars are giving more and more credence to since the notion that Homer's Troy was entirely fictional was disproved seventy years ago and the findings at Crete have given authority to the Minoan labyrinth) that these legends are based on historical fact; the undoubted similarities in character and habit between the people described in the Irish myths and contemporary Mediterranean people, particularly Asiatic Hellenes; the fact that these

1. The First Book of Irish Myths and Legends, Eoin Neeson, Mercier.

Ionians came under the influence of and intermingled with the Scythians of south-east Europe; and that throughout the Irish myths references are continually made (though dismissed by workers such as Eleanor Hull as errors) to Scythia and the visits of Irish heros to the Scythians.

Much capital has been made by philologists tracing the origins of the early Irish by pointing out the variations in the Celtic tongue spoken in Ireland, Wales and Brittany. They use this as the basis for an argument that *all* Celts came across Europe from the region Hungary/Austria/Switzerland. Well, as Aldous Huxley said on one occasion: 'There is an intrinsic plausibility in any explanation of the diverse in terms of a single principle.' It seems to me, in the light of the bulk of circumstantial evidence to the contrary that it is infinitely more likely that the Celtic, or Celtic Scythian, people took off in several directions at the same time. That one group should have reached the Atlantic seabord at Brittany speaking a dialect of their own, while another should have done so via Macedonia, Ionia, Italy, Spain and Ireland speaking another dialect seems to be at least as reasonable on its own merits apart altogether from ancillary evidence, as that a single group from a single source should have reached Brittanny by land, gone from thence to Britain and Wales and thence to Ireland where they not only altered their method of speech significantly, but also infused their tradition with some migrant vitality so that it produced a culture and sophistication which was to prove more superior and more lasting than either of the other two.

Finally, on this point, Herodotus in The Histories, Book 2, points out that certain Ionian colonists in Italy during the second millenium B.C. brought with them a native tongue; but that some centuries later it differed from that of later Ionian colonists somewhat further south but coming from the same source, in much the same way that the language spoken by the Irish differed from that of the Welsh; particularly in the pronunciation of G, K, P and Q.

The first Ionian colonists, by the way, settled in Lombardy close to the area where the transalpine Celts might have trekked towards Brittany; the second group of Ionians were the Milesians en route to Tartessia in Spain, and, it seems possible, to Ireland.

The general assumption that several races of distinct peoples coming from various sources – the Parthalonians, the Nemedians, the Tuatha de Danaans and the Milesians – reached Ireland in successive waves is taken for granted by most scholars. But, on the general body of evidence frail though much of it might be, and more especially on patterns of human behaviour elsewhere but in similar situations, it seems more likely that these peoples who undoubtedly came in successive waves *did so from a common source*. The pattern of migration and colonisation throughout recorded history indicates that it is generally by successive waves of people from the same place of origin that new territories are discovered and developed. The indications are clear enough, although they have been ignored by many, that this is the pattern followed by the early Irish settlers. The exceptions to the rule in this case are the Firbolgs and the Fomorians, but it is made abundantly clear in our tales that this is so. The differences in language, customs and outward character are no doubt what have prevented this hypothesis being accepted; and no doubt in a contemporary context it seems incredible that such variations could exist among the same peoples. But replace these peoples in their native context and they fit into a period of rapid development and mutation spanning about 2,000 years. Such variations not only could, but must, have existed even in people of the same blood living at opposite ends of the world and coming together in wave after wave, no doubt inspired to do so by the tales and traditions of their Phoenician forefathers.

No intelligent person nowadys takes literally racial names such as Slav, Anglo-Saxon, Latin, Celt etc. as an index of (sole) origin. Is there any reason why what is true of to-day should be less true of four thousand years ago when vast migrant bodies of people, apart from the intermingling races of Asia Minor and the Mediterranean, crossed and recrossed the known world and penetrated the unknown? If not, then history, human nature and Nietzsche's master-race concept must have been wrong, unnaturally disciplined and wildly anticipatory in that order.

Additional bits of evidence in support of this theory – given more fully in the introduction to the *First Book of Myths and Legends* – keep turning up. For example in all the Irish legends the heroes are accustomed to rely on their spears, usually described as 'great' and 'small' (see *Diarmuid and Graine* and *The Sickbed of Cuchulain*) as their principal weapons. This presumably refers to a heavy hand spear for close combat of the type universally used in Mediterranean regions since the fourth millenium, and a form of javelin; these javelins, by the way, were carried in a sort of quiver attached to their chariots, an Asia Minor custom. *Always* the method of throwing is described as being done by fitting the (fore)finger into a cord or loop to hurl the spear. In support of the theory that the Celts or Gaels are of Milesian or Phoenician origin (bearing in mind the close association between these peoples and the Scythians) I quote from Professor Yigael Yadin, Professor of Archaeology in the Hebrew University of Jerusalem and who, incidentally, was responsible for the partial excavation of Masada over the past three years (*The Art of Warfare in Biblical Lands*): 'The Bible likens the shaft of Goliath's javelin (Goliath being, it will be recalled, a Phoenician or, in Yadin's terms, one of the 'Seapeople') to a 'weaver's beam', for this type had not been seen in Israel and had no name in Hebrew. What was meant by 'weaver's beam' is the leash rod of a loom. This is a block of wood which separates the threads of the warp to offer passage for the threads of the weft. The characteristic feature was the loop or leashes of cord attached to it ...a typical Aegean javelin has a loop and a cord wound round the shaft so that the weapon could be hurled a greater distance with greater stability by virtue of the resultant spin. The Greeks called such a javelin 'the loop'.' (op. cit. 354/5)

On this particular point it is of some interest to note that in a portrait of Captain Thomas Henry Lee, an Irish soldier, painted in 1594, he is shown holding what appears to be a form of javelin in his right hand with the index finger inserted through a loop. However this is very much later than our period, and by this time it was standard and ubiquitous practice for javelins to have similar loops. However, since the Gaelic tradition (of which the myths and legends, the Brehon law and the social system were the most tenacious aspects) was still surviving, even if in a period of transition, it is not unlikely that tradition in the military sphere excercised some influence also. The portrait, for example, clearly shows that in the matter

10

of dress (which is elaborate and extravagantly decorated in the manner of the period) the Irish tradition was still strong, although the gallant captain wears at his belt an excellent example of a contemporary snaphaunce pistol.

There is a great deal more which could be said and used to illustrate the point – the survival quality of the Gealic tradition which has been evident for more than fifteen hundred years. Is it supposed that it materialised from nothing, out of nowhere, matured and fully sophisticated? Or that it was solely the product of unknown imaginations boiling in the westernmost island of Europe when the entire continent slept after the fall of Rome? Hardly; in broad outline the theory proposed is that these legends are based, however modulated they may have become in the process of verbal and literal passage through time, on historical fact; and that the historical facts on which they are based have too much in common with the spirit and traditions of the Hellenic people of the eastern Mediterranean to have been an accident or to be ignored.

There are three stories in this book, one itself a trilogy. It is a fanciful, half other world tale that has a good deal of poignancy and considerable literary merit – The Children of Lir. But it has been debased by being used as a children's fairy tale for generations. There is also the great epic of the Fenian cycle, *Diarmuid and Graine,* which is to its time and place what *Deirdre and the Sons of Usna* is to the Red Branch cycle and what *Helen and Paris* is to the Iliad. The Fenian cycle is of considerably later date than the Red Branch tales and deals, one is well-satisfied, with undisputedly historical characters. The stories, while transcending human limitations in many respects, cling tenaciously – almost self-consciously – to an everyday context and exaggeratedly recognisable human traits. To draw an extreme example the difference between the two cycles is – to me at any rate – as if one had been written under the influence of a strict all-powerful, but fatherly monarchical society in which all the noble virtues (and all the nobles vices) played a large and intrinsic part, and the other written by the same people some hundreds of years later after they had come under the influence of a considerably, and consciously, more socialised community in which the voice of the lesser blood (not, perhaps, that exactly of the common people, but certainly that of the un-aristocratic middleclass) was loud and powerful.

The time-element alone hardly seems reason enough for such a profound change in approach and it may be that the Fenian cycle was, indeed, the product of some revolutionary change in the social system which required a body of literature of its own. Like many of the myths and legends of both cycles, the story of *Diarmuid and Graine* has more than one version, but the principal source is the Book of Leinster.

The third story in this book comes also from the Red Branch cycle and is another tale about its great hero, Cuchulain, probably the greatest symbol of heroism associated with Ireland. However, in this particular venture, his honour (as the word would probably be interpreted to-day; but notions of honour, whatever about honourableness, like notions of fashion change with the passage of time and what is acceptable to-day may be scandalous to-morrow); his honour, as I said, in this story emerges to-day in a doubtful light because of the manner in which he treats the women who love him. The one, his wife, he lies to blandly; and the other, his mistress, he abandons – albeit with a show of profound grief. However, it is the man, and not the women who are of importance in this story. Nevertheless, in common with other tales from the same cycle, the sophisticated concepts of human behaviour painted with such skill and acute observation are far ahead of their time in Western Europe.

Again, of course, there are several versions of the tale to choose from and there is a discrepancy in the two principal versions, that of the eleventh century *Leabhar na h-Uidri* which has been taken from the earlier and lost *Yellow Book of Slane* which, in turn had two versions to draw on; and a fifteenth century MS in Trinity College, Dublin. The versions differ in many respects. The eleventh century version, for example appears to begin abruptly after the story had already advanced considerably, while the other version does not supply a full conclusion to the tale. The significance, to my mind, of these discrepancies and of the variety of versions of many of these legends lies not in any scholarly detection in trying to trace the 'true' original; but in the fact that so early, which is yet quite late in the literary tradition associated with the tales (we are given to understand), there were so many

12

versions, clearly an index to the additional fact that there *must* have been several oral versions at an even earlier date. The inference to be drawn from this within the context of my argument is that it supports, not the retelling of an artificial composition (so much less likely to literary mutation), but the transmitting of something far more personal, and in which the listeners could be far more personally involved, the histories of their ancestors. In the telling and retelling of something believed, or half believed, and based on fact the room for expansion; for glorification; for heroic dimension is clearly far more readily available than in the case of mere fiction. Any parent knows that a slip in the retelling of a favourite fairy tale, be it just a matter of a word, and all hell breaks loose; but the tendency to aggrandise the feats and stature of our ancestors is inherent in all of us, and the more of us there are telling the stories about them, the more variations of the stories there will be.

In *The Sickbed of Cuchulain*, the row of asterisks signifies the point at which the two versions coincide in the tale.

However, the principal purpose of these myths and legends is enjoyment and enrichment and, I hope, some little additional knowledge into the lives and customs of the people who lived in Ireland between four and one thousand years ago. Apart from the Greek and Roman myths there is not a literature in Europe so old on which to draw, nor one nearly as old which is the product of so advanced a society – barbaric though that society may appear to us in many respects now.

Eoin Neeson
Dublin, 1965

The Children of Lir

At the battle of Tailteann, that was fought so long ago that no one now could tell you very much about it save its name and location and about that they might even be doubtful, the Milesians who brought with them the modern wonders of the eastern world, overcame the Tuatha de Danaan who clung to the older and more mystic ways, and wrested from them the lordship over all of Ireland. And it is not known whether that battle at Tailteann, which was the place of hosting each year for the great games like those held across the ocean on the Corinthian Isthmus; it is not known whether that battle was one of blood and carnage and death and destruction on the jagged battlefield, or of honoured and symbolic victory on the sculptured field of sport. All that is known is that at Tailteann the Milesians were victorious over the de Danaan, but that they subsequently held them in high esteem for their knowledge, wisdom and command of mysteries, while they themselves took over the duties of administering the country.

As time passed the Milesians became more and more the people of the world, active and vigorous, whose minds were turned towards the future and its development, and the Tuatha de Danaan receded more and more into a world of mystery and of imagination where they were their own lords and masters. And so each side conceded to the other what was of least significance to itself, and gained from the other what was of most importance to itself, which was a very sensible arrangement... for it is unknown the number of wars and disputes; countless the amount of blood spilled and bodies mutilated, for want of a few people having the good sense to exchange something of little value to them, instead of holding fast to something that is of little value to them but of great value to another, merely because they happen to have it.

In any event, the de Danaan retreated from the world which the Milesians charged at so successfully, and cultivated their skills as magicians and spirit people and soon inhabited a world parallel to, but quite apart from, that inhabited by the Milesians. And for their great powers and because of their ability in these fields, which the Milesians respected greatly and stood in awe of, they were paid considerable honour and acknowledgement from the newcomers.

But, before all this happened and after the defeat at Tailteann, the de Danaans from the five provinces of all Ireland assembled together to choose a king to rule over them, for their leaders were of one mind that it was no longer to their advantage, but greatly to their disadvantage, to be divided and split up into separate communities each owing its allegiance to one lord or prince, so that there was no common purpose among them except when all were in peril – and even then it wasn't always too easy to put them of one mind about a thing.

So the chiefs and lords, of whom there were many, decided that they would have a single king above the others to rule over them and to provide a common leader, lawgiver and seat of justice for all and they went into conclave to elect such a one. Now of all the chiefs there were five from whom the king would be chosen. These were the greatest and most powerful chiefs among them; also the wisest and most respected and they were the two sons of the Dagda, Eoai Ollamh oracle and once great king of all the de Danaan for more than seventy years, but who had been wounded so severely at the second Battle of Moytura with the Firbolgs and Fomorians (wounded, indeed, by Caitlin, the buck-toothed wife of Balor of the Evil Eye himself) that he died shortly afterwards in his palace at the Boyne, Brugh na Boinne. His two sons were Aengus Og, who himself lived now at Brugh na Boinne, and Bodbh Dearg, the great king of Connacht who had been attacked by the Fomorians and Firbolgs so that it sparked off that same battle of Moytura in which his father was fatally wounded, and into which Lugh Lamh Fada came to help beat the Fomorians. But that story is told elsewhere.[1] Aengus had no wish to be king as he preferred to stay at Brugh na Boinne, where he could pursue his interests in the wisdom and learning of the race, in which he was the most skilled of all. Also candidates for the high office were Ilbrec of Assaroe, of whom little is known at all, Midhir the Proud

1. The First Book of Irish Myths and Legends, by Eoin Neeson, Mercier Press.

of Bri-Leith whose tale is also told elsewhere and Lir of Sidhe Fionna, and it is with Lir and what happened after the conclave that our story properly begins.

The chiefs, all except the five named above, went into solemn session and debated who would be king above them all. The decision they arrived at, at long last, was that the most proper and fitting person for the high place was the Bodbh Dearg of Connacht, son of the great Dagda. But when the result of their deliberations became known all the candidates were pleased and overjoyed that the Bodbh Dearg was elected – all, that is, but one; and that one was Lir of Sidhe Fionna who took the election of another as a personal affront. He was filled with anger and envy, so certain was he that none but himself would have been considered, and when the truth became known he rose up in a white blaze of anger and straightaway left the assembly, not speaking a word to a man, nor showing any mark of respect or homage to the new king.

His ill-mannered behaviour angered the other chiefs who would have sent troops against his fortress at Sidhe Fionna, which was in the county Monaghan near Newtown Hamilton, to burn it and destroy it and kill Lir himself for his ignorant and ill-bred ways, and because he had not submitted to their king elected freely by their council and with his own agreement as well as theirs.

But Bodbh Dearg prevented them.

'Lir,' he said, 'is a powerful man and now an embittered one too. If we attempt to reduce him by force he will defend his territory and many will be killed; but the result will not make me any more your king than I am now, even though he has not submitted to me.'

The lords and chiefs of the de Danaan were impressed with the wisdom and justice of what he said and matters were allowed to rest thus for some time. The Bodbh Dearg ruled over the de Danaan from his palace at Killaloe and Lir lived with his people in isolation and bitterness at Sidhe Fionna. But, in the midst of his loneliness, for it was a lonely stand he had taken where none of the de Danaan other than his own people would associate with him, a new misfortune struck him. His wife died suddenly after an illness that lasted only three days. She was a young and beautiful woman much respected throughout the whole country and the event caused a considerable stir among the de Danaan when they heard of it. When the news reached Killaloe, indeed, where the great Bodbh Dearg was sitting in court with his nobles, the king was moved to compassion at the misfortune of Lir.

'It is at a time such as this,' he told the assembled company, 'that a man stands most in need of friendship, and for Lir, where he is in Sidhe Fionna, separated from his peers, the warm hand of friendship has long been a stranger. Now that his wife is dead my friendship would be of service to him, if he would accept it. As you know,' he went on, 'I am foster-father to the three beautiful daughters of Aillil, king of the Islands of Aran, who are with us here in Killaloe, Niamh, Aoife and Albha, the most accomplished as well as among the most beautiful women in Erin and Lir would be foolish if he spurned my offer of friendship now.'

The de Danaan again agreed that the king's wisdom was great and his nobility warm and messengers were accordingly sent to Lir at Sidhe Fionna. They took with them the following message:

'Lir, Lord of Sidhe Fionna, Chief of the de Danaan of Frewen, greetings; If you will submit to the king, the Bodbh Dearg, he will give you for a wife one of his three foster-children, the daughters of Aillil of Aran, and his friendship forever.'

When Lir recieved this message he was pleased. He was bored with lack of congenial companionship and had had time to get over his annoyance at not being elected to the kingship; furthermore alliance with the king, as he considered it, both in friendship and by ties of marriage, was not to be lightly considered. He therefore set out for Killaloe on the following day with a retinue of fifty chariots and they never stopped nor turned aside on their journey from Sidhe Fionna until they reached the palace of the Bodbh Dearg. They were greeted with great enthusiasm by the king and his chiefs, for they were all happy to see the breach in the ranks of the de Danaan healed and though Lir had not at first submitted to the king, he was a good, if proud, man, held in high esteem by his fellows and by the king himself... therefore he was welcomed with due ceremony, he made his acknowledgements to the king, and that night they were entertained at a banquet given by the people of the Tuatha, the De and the Dan – the

18

entire company of the Tuatha de Danaan, who were at Killaloe.

And it might well be a good thing to explain here that there are many notions of how the Tuatha de Danaan achieved their name. Some say that they brought it with them from the eastern world where they had their origin, some say that they are named after the three sons of Danaan, Brian and Iuchair and Iucharbha and so called because they were skilled in wisdom and magic, and so were known as Tuatha or sorcerers. But it is hard to believe, for they brought with them to Ireland their sorcery from the east. Others say that they were so-called because they were three distinct tribes, but that is a fanciful notion; while the truth, so far as we know it at all, is that they were one people of three parts, or three estates, it might be held to-day – such as we all are, indeed, for man has not changed very much for all the time he's been here to think – and the first estate was that of the leaders and nobility, for Tuath is the name of a lord; and the second estate were the De, or gods; the druids and magicans, and the third estate were the Dan, the artificers and craftsmen. And it was the representatives of the three estates that gave to the lord Lir a noble banquet when he arrived at Killaloe to make submission to the king of the Tuatha de Danaan.

Next day Lir went to the great hall where the Bodbh Dearg sat on his throne with his queen beside him; and beside them both were their three foster-daughters, Niamh, Aoife and Arbha. And the Bodbh Dearg said to Lir:

'These are my foster-daughters, the most beautiful and most accomplished among all the women of Ireland. Take your choice among them and whichever you choose, she will be your wife.'

Lir looked at them with wonder. For they were all beautiful, and none more beautiful than another. Niamh, the eldest, had the beauty of the winter about her, for her hair was as dark as the trees of the forest against the deep snow lying about their feet, and her skin was as white as that snow that stretches, smooth and gentle, above the bones of the earth. Her eyes were dark and sparkling like the frosted night, and her body was as beautiful, slender and well-shaped, as a doe in November.

Aoife, the second daughter of the king of Aran, was like

the beauty of the Autumn; her hair was dark russet with the glint of gold in it and her skin was the colour of cream from a richly fed cow; her eyes were hazel with green flecks in them and her form was soft and voluptuous with the ripeness of youth, while the third daughter, Albha had the beauty of spring, so young and fresh and fair was she, but she has no part in this story, so it is sufficient to say that she was as beautiful as her sisters, and leave it at that. With their beauty the three maidens combined intelligence, charm and wit and Lir found it impossible to choose one of them for her own sake. Therefore he said:

'They are all beautiful, but to choose one of them is beyond me for I cannot say which of the three is best.' (And in this he showed a wisdom, perhaps, derived from one of his Hellenic forbears called Paris, who, when he found himself in a somewhat similar situation displayed the bad judgement of making a distinction.)

'Therefore,' went on Lir, 'I will take the eldest, for she must be the most fitting to be wife to a chief of the de Danaan.'

The king agreed and with tremendous pomp and ceremony the wedding was arranged and celebrated. The newly married couple remained at Killaloe for a month and then left for Sidhe Fionna and Lir's castle, where the marriage was celebrated all over again with a great wedding feast at which the nobles and kings of Ireland were made welcome.

Lir and Niamh were happy at Sidhe Fionna where they lived in comfort and in friendliness with everyone now that Lir and the Bodbh Dearg were reunited. In the course of time Niamh bore children to Lir, twins, and they were called Finola and Aedh; and they were fine, healthy children who grew fat and pink in the grianan of Sidhe Fionna until they were a year old, when their mother again gave birth to twins, two boys this time, called Fiachra and Conn; but unhappiness and tragedy arrived with the birth of these two sons, for Niamh, died in giving them birth, and for a second time Lir was left without a wife to love and to love him. So great was his anguish and despair that he nearly died of the vast grief that consumed him and only his great love for his children turned his mind from the sorrow that lived within him.

When the news of this new tragedy reached Killaloe the

grief of the Bodbh Dearg was scarcely less than that of Lir himself, and the people of his household raised a great wail of sorrow and loss for Niamh which lasted for a fortnight. When their period of mourning was over, the king assembled them in the great hall and said:

'We have been afflicted with a terrible sorrow and loss in the death of Niamh, and we grieve for her both on our own account and for the sake of the noble to whom we gave her, for we acknowledge his alliance and friendship. But it is in our heart, and in our power, to alleviate his sorrow and in so doing to soften our own and cement the ties between us with an even stronger bond, for I will give him her sister for a wife, my second foster-child Aoife.'

Messengers were again sent to Sidhe Fionna to tell Lir of the king's decision. Lir received them and their message with affection and with sadness in equal parts; affection because of the king's nobility of mind, and sadness because he had loved Niamh so well and felt her loss so deeply. Nevertheless after a period of mourning he went to Killaloe to the king's palace where he and Aoife were married and united, and after the wedding he brought her home with him to Sidhe Fionna.

Now Aoife did not have the blessing of children of her own as her years with Lir accumulated and grew; but that did not unduly trouble her, for she loved her husband greatly, and gave to his children the love which she would have given to children of her own. She cared for them with great tenderness and, indeed, her love for them increased every day that the sun rose upon the world. In fact, the whole race of the de Danaan, loved these lovely children, who were their joy and their delight, for those who saw them were captured by their beauty and their gentleness – which is a thing rare enough in many children nowadays, thanks to the fact that it is even rarer in their elders – and could not help loving them with their whole heart. The king himself loved them with the love of a grandfather and went frequently to Sidhe Fionna to visit them; and when he was not thinking of going to Lir's castle to see them and bring them gifts, he was thinking of bringing them to Killaloe and assembling gifts there for them, where he kept them for as long as possible and was a sadder and an older man each time they had to leave to go home again.

Now, at this time the Tuatha de Danaan celebrated the

Feast of Gobhann which was a notable occasion dedicated to their power over sickness, decay and old age and instituted by Manannan Mac Lir. Now Manannan was not the son of our Lir, but of a much older origin, and had at this time assumed the stature of a god among the people of the Tuatha de Danaan. The Feast of Gobhann was a ceremony which ensured that the people of the Tuatha de Danaan would join the Marcra Sidhe, or Mystic Cavalcade in the Tir Tairrngire, or Land of Promise, called Tir na nOg or Land of Youth by those who don't know any better. And the Feast was celebrated at the houses of different chiefs in turn. It was when it was celebrated in the castle of Lir that the hosts of the de Danaan came to know and love the children of Lir. And as they did so, the pride and love of their father in them grew as well, and it was a delight to see how it showed in him. The four little children slept close by him; and he would often rise from his bed at the dawn of the day and go to them to talk with them and to play with them before the work of the day began. But it was this very delight in and love for his children that brought great sorrow in its train.

Aoife, perhaps feeling the years of her youth flying from her – but why she should feel thus is a mystery, since the Feast of Gobhann was as beneficient to the women of the de Danaan as to the men – or perhaps feeling the deep ache in her rich body, that is the ache of a yearning but infecund woman, when she saw those children receiving such attention from their father and from all the others who came to the castle, began to fancy that she was neglected on their account. The barb of unreason, jealousy, lodged in her heart, and she began to seek for reasons on which it might take hold; suspicion provides its own reasons and envy its own logic, and it did not take long for the love that she had felt and lavished upon them to turn to hatred which fed upon their happiness.

CHAPTER TWO

Aoife's jealousy became such an obsession with her that she became ill, not only sick and ill in her mind, but in her body too as the torment of the one was transferred to the other. For a year she lay in bed, full of bitterness and brooding evil, and her speech and appearance were attributed to her sickness of body for which there appeared to be no remedy. Her sickness worried Lir, who had already lost two wives, a great deal and he paid her much attention, but even this did not offset Aoife's jealousy, but rather fed it, as she considered he turned to her only out of pity. However, at the end of a year, she had reached a decision and made it known that she was well and arose from her sickbed.

She called the children to her and told them that to celebrate her recovery she was going to take them on a visit to their foster-grandfather, the king Bodbh Dearg at Killaloe. They were delighted, of course – all except Finola, who had dreamed on the previous night a dark dream of foreboding in which Aoife had perpetrated some dreadful deed on herself and her brothers. Finola was afraid that their step-mother intended some harm to them, even though it was only a dream she had, and did not want to go. Nevertheless she was persuaded, since she was ashamed to speak her fears in case she would be laughed at and thought ungrateful.

Aoife ordered her carriages and chariots to be harnessed and, with her personal servants as guards, she set out from Sidhe Fionna for Killaloe with the children. They had not gone very far when she called aside one of her most trusted retainers, and said to him:

'You love me well, Conan, or is it just that you are my servant?'

'You know me better than that,' he replied indignantly, 'didn't I come from Aran with you when you were only a small child and haven't I watched over every hair of your head since then in case any harm would befall you?'

'Then you do love me?' she asked.

'There isn't a thing in the world I wouldn't do for you,' he said.

'Good,' replied Aoife, 'and if I was in any danger, or suffering from a great loss what would you do about it?'

'Remove the one and restore the other if I had to face the battlefields of the world to do it,' he answered, and that satisfied her.

'Well then,' she said, 'listen to me. I am losing the love of my husband.'

'Glory be to God,' he replied, 'is that a fact? Is it another woman or what? Tell me her name and it's the end of her.'

''Tis no woman has me neglected in his eyes and forsaken in his house,' she said, 'but those children you see there before you. They have me destroyed and ruined and my life blighted and if you were to remove them and kill them out of my sight, I will reward you with what wealth your heart may desire.'

But Conan looked at her in horror as she spoke, and rage welled up in her at his look, for she could not understand the cause of it so blinded was she with her hate and jealousy, thinking that she could not be wrong and that therefore all things she would do were justifiable; she raged at his stupidity, but could do nothing about it. Conan in his horror backed away from her silently and no more was said between them about it.

And it was the same with those others of her retainers that she approached. One and all they refused with contempt and horror on their faces and lips, warning her that evil would certainly follow her for the thing she contemplated.

Then, in her rage, she took a sword in her hand and determined to kill them herself, but her deep womanly instincts came between her and her hatred, and prevented her. So they set out once again and continued their journey until they came to the shores of Lough Derravaragh in Westmeath, where they made a camp and sat about while a meal was being prepared.

With a smile of false friendship on her face Aoife led the children to the lakeside and suggested that they have a bathe while they waited for the meal; delighted they threw off their costly clothing and ran into the water with childish shouts of joy, but, one by one as they passed her, Aoife struck them with a golden druidical wand and transformed them into four, beautiful, snow white swans. Then she spoke to them these words:

'Fly to your homes on Derravarragh's shore
And with its clamouring birds protest your fate;
Your friends may seek to find you evermore
In vain, now I have satisfied my burning hate.'

The four bewildered and frightened children fluttered this way and that way in the shallows of the lake in frantic efforts to shake off their carapace of snow-white feathers, soft as a whispered word on a pillow on the outside, but, for them who were captured within as hard as the forged and ringing iron bars of a prison cell.

Finally they quietened down and added to that sad dignity of all swans the immeasurable sadness that now descended on them as they realised the full extent of their plight.

Finola who, like the other children, still possessed the power of speech, like them turned her face towards their stepmother, and spoke for all of them: 'Oh, Aoife,' she said, 'why did you do this terrible thing to us? Your friendship for us has turned out to be the friendship of a traitor and you have destoyed us without a cause that we can see. But what you've done will cry out for vengeance for as many years as vengeance takes to reach you; your power is not greater than the power of the Tuatha de Danaan and their punishment, Aoife, you may be sure, will be that much greater than ours as yours now is greater than what we were.'

And having said this the children together made this song:

'You, who loved us in the days that fled
Down the vortex of sweet things, now dead;
Who summoned up those old and horrid words
In newborn hate, that wrought us into birds,
Have cast aside that fostered love you bore
And hurled us forth, from storm to stormy shore.'

Finola, when they had finished this song, turned again to Aoife and said: 'Tell us one thing at least, how long shall we be in the shape of swans, so that we may know when our misery will end?'

Aoife smiled grimly at her: 'You'd have been wiser not to have asked that question,' she said, 'but since you have asked it then I'll tell you the truth, and may it be a solace or an anger to you as you wish; three hundred years you'll spend, on lake Derravarragh; three hundred more on the Sea of Moyle between Ireland and Scotland; three hundred years in Erris and Inis Glora on the Western Sea... as many years you will spend until the union of Lairgnean, the prince of the north, with Deichthe, the princess of the south; until the Taill-ceann comes to Ireland from abroad, bringing with him a new belief in the word of God come to earth... and neither by your own power, or by my power or the power of your friends can you be freed until the time comes.'

But now that she had spoken the words, the venom and the bitterness that was in her heart flew with them out of her mouth and she repented what she had done; it was as if the release of the words themselves released also the jealous hate in her, and she said:

'Since I cannot give you anything else, I'll grant you the power to keep your human speech; and your voices will be so sweet that you will sing music sweeter than any music heard in the world before and which will lull into sleep all who listen to it. Moreover you will keep your human intelligence and will not be sad any longer for being in the shape of swans.'

> 'Fly from me you gentle swans
> And make your home on the restless waves,
> Build your nest on the ocean's breast
> Drape yourself in its snowywhite crest,
> Find shelter in deep-bitten caves.
>
> Fly from me you drifting swans
> And fill with music and ancient songs
> Derravarragh's wind-swept shore,
> The coasts where endless oceans roar,
> A thousand years will not seem long.
>
> Unhappy Lir, in grief and pain
> Your names may call across the world.
> His sundered heart will halt and fail –
> His empty hearth repeat the wail –
> On me his vengeance shall be hurled.

Across the margins of an age
Your agony no hand may cease
Until across the narrowing sea
Will come the Word of Him who'll be
For all the succour and release.'

Then, Aoife, her face hardened again with her own determination and the knowledge that she was committed to an unalterable course, turned away from the lakeside and ordered her horses to be yoked to her chariot again. She left the four swans together on the lonely lake behind her, swimming aimlessly close to the shore. Their own sorrow was enormous, for they were still children thrown athwart the world for a bitter age. But they made this song, thinking of the sorrow of their father:

'Our hearts break for our sad father
Searching the world with sick eyes,
Leaping at shadows in lands and skies
Seeking his children, wrenched from his home.
Four swans adrift on the voiceless foam,
Treading the water for evermore,
Flying from the storms to a cold shore.'

When Aoife reached Killaloe and the palace of the Bodbh Dearg, she was given a tremendous welcome, for the news of her sickness had gone before her, but not that of her recovery, and her foster-father received her with great joy. After he had welcomed her, he asked her why she hadn't brought the children of Lir with her this time.

Now Aoife knew that he would ask her this, and she had prepared her answer on the way – even though she knew it would be found to be untrue in time. But in the manner of all those who have committed an evil, she had no choice but to lie unless she made the truth known, even though she piled another wrong on what she had already done and knew that this would count against her eventually. Still she bought a little time for herself. And so she said:

'I did not bring them because Lir is no longer your friend and ally. He has turned against you, as he has turned against me, and will not trust his children to you in case you would do them harm.'

The Bodbh Dearg was, naturally, astonished at this, for he was aware that Lir knew he loved the children as if they were really his grandchildren, and not just the children of his own foster-child. 'How could that be,' he asked her, 'I love those children as I love my own.'

Now he was no fool. He questioned Aoife further, but the vagueness and discrepancies of her answers only made him all the more uneasy. He suspected that something was wrong from her attitude, but had no idea what it might be. Secretly, therefore he sent messengers northwards to Sidhe Fionna to enquire for the children and to ask that they might come on a visit to him with their foster-mother.

When the messengers arrived and told this to Lir he, in his turn, was astonished and upset.

'But didn't they reach Killaloe with Aoife,' he asked, 'they certainly left here with her for the Bodbh Dearg's palace.'

The messengers answered:

'Aoife arrived alone, and she told the king that you refused to allow the children to come.'

Lir didn't know what to make of this. With his mind in a turmoil he first of all raged at the messengers that they were fools and liars, but they eventually convinced him of the truth of what they said. This only made him worse, for he could not understand why Aoife should say this to the king. He loved her and trusted her and she had never lied to him or shown any duplicity before towards him or anyone else so far as he knew. Then he thought of her illness, which was inexplicable, and the thought struck him with terror that her mind had become deranged and that she had murdered the children while in that condition. In terror and distraction he ordered his chariots to be yoked and, with whatever men he could lay his hands on, set out immediately for Killaloe, covering every inch of the ground they passed on the way. Slowly, for the mind of Lir was burdened as it had never been before, they came towards Lough Derravarragh.

The four swans who had been left there by Aoife were swimming silently a little way from the shore, just outside a sprouting bank of reeds, when the cavalcade topped a hill above the lake. Finola was the first to see it, and she sang, with all the power of music and song that Aoife had left them:

> 'Over the hilltop and down to the lake
> Slowly and sadly the warriors make
> A path through the heather and by the wild shore;
> Tardy the wheels now of chariots that sped
> And heavy the feet of the soldiers who bore
> Our parents past here when first they were wed.
>
> Their hearts are dull, dull too their shields;
> Dull their eyes that reap shorn fields,
> The royal hosts of de Danaan
> Under skies of changing hue
> Seeking us from dawn to dawn,
> Who've found us here, and lost us too.'

When Lir and his men came to the shore and heard the swans speaking in human voices, they wondered greatly at this miracle and stopped. Lir walked to the waters' edge, his heart thumping within him, for he knew that this strangeness was no small thing and sensed that it would mean much to him. He spoke to the swans and asked them how it was they had human voices.

'Oh dear father,' cried Finola, 'you do not know us. I am Finola, and these your other children, changed to swans and ruined by the hatred and witchcraft of Aoife, our own mother's sister, and your wife.'

When Lir heard this he gave three great cries of grief and lamentation and looked as if he would lose his reason altogether in his sorrow. After a while he recovered sufficiently to ask them:

'How can I restore you to your proper form? What must I do?'

'Nothing,' replied Finola, 'no one has the power to release us for more than a thousand years. Until Lairgnean the prince from the north and Deichthe the princess from the south are united.'

When they heard this Lir and all his people again raised three shouts of lamentation. Their grief was lifted by the wind and carried across the face of Ireland until the trees bent beneath it, and the waves beating her shores receded from it.

When they had become silent again, and their silence was like the dropping of snow after the thunder of their grief, Lir said:

'You still have your speech and your reason, so let you come to land and you can live with us at Sidhe Fionna, talking and behaving as if you still had your proper shapes.'

'That is not possible either,' cried Finola, 'we are condemned to inhabit the waters of the lake and can not live with human people any more. Aoife has only allowed us to keep our minds and our speech, and we have the power to make music so sweet that those who hear it will never desire any other happiness.'

Lir and his people stayed by the lakeside that night and the four children of Lir sang and made music for them so that they were lulled into a calm, gentle sleep as they listened and their cares and worries fell from them. But as dawn broke over the low hills to the east, Lir stood up, and slowly walked again to the water's edge to say goodbye to his children while he went to search for Aoife:

'Broken the heart in my bonded breast
That I must leave you children here
Far from where your heads sought rest;
Far from the empty halls of Lir.

I curse the day that first I saw
Aoife's smiling face that screened
A cruelty no love might thaw
Like poison in a cup concealed.

I know no rest, I know no sleep
For through the never ending night
I glimpse the children I would keep
Forever in my fading sight.

Finola, daughter of my heart,
Proud Aedh than whom was none more bold,
Fiachra, gentler that the hart,
And little Conn – more dear than gold –

Oh, here on Derravarragh's shore
Trapped by Aoife's evil power...
Oh God! My children! Never more
Will Lir enjoy a tranquil hour.'

When Lir left he travelled directly to Killaloe, where he was welcomed. He said nothing of what he knew, but greeted the king and Aoife without showing his feelings. The Bodbh Dearg then began to reproach him for not bringing the children with him, and all the while Aoife was standing beside him.

Then Lir turned and looked directly at his wife. She looked back at his expressionless face for a moment, and then dropped her gaze. Lir turned back again to the king.

'It was not I who prevented my children from coming to stay with you, Bodbh Dearg,' he said, 'but Aoife, your own foster-child and sister of their mother. She has turned on them and treacherously turned them into four swans, now trapped in Lough Derravarragh.'

At first the Bodbh Dearg didn't believe Lir. He could not understand how one of his own foster-children, on whom he had lavished love and attention, could do such a thing. He turned to her, wordlessly, for a denial, but when he saw the expression on her face, he realised that what Lir had said was the truth.

'Aoife...' was all he could say, and it was as much an appeal to prove Lir wrong, as a shocked reaction to what he said. But there was no movement from Aoife, who looked stonily before her, knowing that the vengeance she had tried to avoid had come upon her all the quicker.

The Bodbh Dearg drew himself up and terrible he looked in his tormented anger.

When he spoke his voice was low and fierce:

'What you have done,' he said, 'will be worse for you than for the children you have harmed, for their suffering will come to an end and they will find happiness at last.'

Then for a while he stayed looking at her with a frown of awful anger and justice on his face. When he spoke his voice was even fiercer than it had been before.

'Of all that is on the earth, or above it, or beneath it; of all that flies or creeps or burrows, seen or unseen, horrible in

31

itself or in its nature, what do you most abhor?'

Now it was incumbent on Aoife that certain questions put to her must be answered truthfully, for she was under an obligation older than the Tuatha de Danaan itself to do so and if she did not the fate that would befall her would be worse and more lasting than any fate that mere man might devise for her, and so she was forced to answer truthfully. And she said:

'Of all that you have said, the things most loathsome to me are the Morrigu – the demons of the air.'

'That, then, is what you will be,' said the Bodbh Dearg, and as he spoke he struck her with a druidical golden wand, such as the one she had herself used on the children of Lir, and transformed her into one of the dreaded Morrigu, which can take many shapes, and relishes in battle and the spilling blood of men, but is most often seen in the black, and dreaded shape of a croaking raven.

Immediately Aoife was turned into something so horrible and revolting to behold that all those in the great hall of the palace of Killaloe, turned away or hid their faces in their cloaks, save only Lir and the Bodbh Dearg alone who stood and looked at the transformation with imperturbable countenances.

The thing that was now Aoife, crouched low on the floor for a moment, flapping its ugly, leathery wings. Then, with a scream from its gaping mouth, it spread them wide and flew upwards, over the heads of those below who cringed away as it passed above and out through the great door until it disappeared among the clouds in the distance. She had become a demon of the air, a Morrigu; and a demon of the air she remains and will remain until the end of time.

Then the Bodbh Dearg and all his court, and the Tuatha de Danaan from the four corners of Ireland, assembled on the shores of Lough Derravarragh and camped there, that they might remain with the white swans and listen to their music. And there too came the hosts of the Milesians from Tara and their kingly courts and made another camp to listen to the music of the swans. For it is said and written that no music was heard in the world before that, or since, to compare with the music of the swans.

And round the lake there lived and grew a great community

of people bonded together by their love of the swans and the music made by them. During the day the swans would talk with their friends and at night they sang their incomparable music so that all those who heard it, no matter what their grief, or sickness; sorrow or pain, forgot what it was that troubled them and drifted into a gentle sleep from which they woke calm and refreshed. This, then, was how they lived for three hundred years; the de Danaans and the Milesians in their own, vast communities by the lakeside, and the three swans in the shallow water near the lake's edge. At the end of that time Finola said to her brothers:

'The time we were to spend on Lough Derravarragh has come to an end and we have only one more night left to us here, for to-morrow we must leave our friends and our own people and fly from here to the cold sea of Moyle.'

When the three sons of Lir heard this they were disheartened for they were as happy, almost, on the lake and with their own people as if they had lived in Sidhe Fionna where they had been born. Now they were doomed to the dark waves of the Sea of Moyle, threshing its passage between Ireland and Scotland, far from human companionship.

Early the following morning, therefore, in sadness and sorrow, they approached the shore to speak to their father for the last time and to bid their friends farewell. And this is the lament that they sang before they left:

'Tears are swelling in our hearts
As the lake must swell and weep
When time lays down his hand athwart
Its water, calm and deep,
And sunders it and blows black storms
Across its tranquil path;
For we must leave your courts and warmth
And seek the endless wrath
Of Moyle's wild sea; three hundred years
There to linger in our fears.

Far down the twisted roads of time
Our paths ahead are mapped;
Though men may with the fates combine
Our destinies are trapped;
No dreams we dream, no hopes may raise,
No laughter in to-morrow;
Till comes that holy voice of praise
Our lives are doomed to sorrow.
But though we go our hearts remain
To ease your grief and mortal pain.'

Then, as the last notes of their lament died away across the surface of the lake, the four birds, all together, began to skim over the lake, their wings and their feet combining to lift them from the water and their long necks outstretched before them. They lifted gently until their feet were barely running on the surface and then, with powerful sweeps of their broad wings, they abandoned the lake which had been their home for so long and rose upwards into the air. Higher they climbed and higher, making great circles as they rose, the sound of their beating wings coming down clearly to the many thousands of people below. And when the swans had reached a great height, where they could look down and see, not only Derravarragh and the camp of the men of Ireland beside it, but much of the country around as well, they paused in their flight for a moment, and then flew straight northwards, straight and true, until they saw the bitter foam and white savagery of the Sea of Moyle, scouring the ocean bed between Ireland and Scotland, rising ahead. Lower they sank and lower until they touched the first cold wave to reach up for them. Then they landed, awkwardly, on the cruel sea that was to be their new home.

The people of Ireland were so saddened and upset at their departure that they made a law forbidding anyone to kill a swan in Ireland from that time on.

The framing of this legislation and its passing was done in a fervour of activity and energy; the enthusiasm of those who became caught up in it and who supported it was sincere and infectious and carried the wholehearted support of the entire people with it until it became law. But when it was passed, and had become a law of the land, there was no more to be done; gradually it was realised that this made not the slightest difference to the plight of the children of Lir, wild and hot though the enthusiasm had been for the passing of the law. Nor was there anything further that could be done to help them. And so, sadder, wiser perhaps, proud of their unimportant piece of legislation, the people forgot about the Children of Lir, for there was nothing else left for them to do.

All, that is, except Lir himself, the Bodbh Dearg and a few more who had known all along that all the laws in the world won't redress a wrong if equity and justice are not possible, and who loved the Children of Lir for their own sakes and not because they represented anything.

Meanwhile the Children of Lir themselves were adrift on the jagged face of Moyle, tossed from wave to wave by the growling sea. Their own hearts were full of sorrow and sadness for their father and their friends even in their own terrible plight; and when they looked about them, at the dark green-bellied, wild sea, and the steep, rocky, far-stretching coasts they were overcome with fear and despair. Cold and hunger struck at them too, for it was not like the warm, inland, well-stocked waters of pleasant Derravarragh; here the wind swept bitingly down from the north, with sleet and snow in its teeth; the sea harboured little of food in that wild place, and Derravarragh appeared like nothing compared to what they now suffered.

This was how they lived for some time, thinking their lives and misery could never be greater than it was, until one evening that – wintry though it was, with pale, milky clouds stretched coldly across the sky, and the sea heaving restively beneath them – the sky suddenly became darker and seemed to close in about them. They realised a storm was on the way, and Finola said:

'Brothers, this storm has taken us by surprise and we are

35

unprepared for it. It is certain that we will be separated in it so it would be as well if we fixed a meeting place afterwards, otherwise we might never see each other again.'

And Fiachra said: 'That is sensible, so let's meet at Carricknarone, for that is a place we all know well.'

And, for a few hours, they stayed together, huddled in a group on top of the bellowing sea. With midnight came the storm. A wild wind swept across the black sea, roughening the billows, and lightening flashes threw themselves forth from the clouds so that it seemed as if the ocean was under attack from the sky and was rousing itself mightily to fight back, for the sea rose as if from its bed and clawed at the sky with angry fingers of lashing spume. And as the storm grew worse the swans were separated and scattered across the surface of the fighting sea so that not one of them knew in what direction the others had been driven. All through the night they were tossed and hurled, whipped and blown, sometimes in the sea and sometimes in the air and sometimes in a raging mixture of the two, from one place to another place, but never knowing what place they were in. Only with great courage and willpower did they manage to survive at all, and even then they were more dead than alive when the dawn began to lighten the east. With the dawn the storm abated, and by full light the sea was again calm and smooth, but with the troubled look, restless underneath, that it always has after a storm. When she was rested a bit, Finola made her way to Carricknarone. But there was no sign of any of her brothers either on the sullen waves beating about the rock, or on the craggy corners of the rock itself. She climbed to the top of it and looked around over the desolate wastes, but there was still no sign of them. Cold and terrified, she believed them dead, and began to lament them:

> 'There is no shelter, there is no rest,
> My heart is broken in my breast;
> Gone, my three loves in the bitter night;
> Gone, all but the deep, cold fright
> Of despair, and life without light.

My brothers are lost in the wild sea
Where death itself would be a mercy;
Oh, is there no pity in this place?
Will I never see again each face
Dearer now to me than the human race?

There is no shelter, there is no rest,
My heart is broken in my breast;
Was not the agony we bore enough?
Was not the cruelty, the deep trough
Of long anguish sufficient pain to suffer?'

Then she sank down on the rock and buried her head under her wing. Her spirits sank lower and lower, for she believed herself to be alone of the four children of Lir, and wished to die. Finally, when she had made up her mind to accept death, she raised her head to take a last look at the bleak world that she was about to leave. She looked out over the pale sea, almost one colour with the inhospitable sky and there, in the distance, she saw a small speck of bedraggled white being tossed this way and that way by the careless sea, but making its way towards the rock slowly with feeble motions; it was Conn that she saw, and when she recognised him she forgot her terror and despair and plunged into the moving water to help him towards Carricknarone – which is properly called the rock of the seals, for it is there that the seal people congregate when the weather is welcoming. But, needless to remark, there was no sign of life about the rock at this time save for themselves, and the few ravaging sea birds that circled above in search of prey. She helped Conn to the rock and there they rested. Shortly afterwards they saw Fiachra limping through the water, and it took both of them a mighty effort to bring him to safety for he was closer to death than he was to life and when they spoke to him he could not summon up a word or any acknowledgement whatsoever in return, and so Finola and Conn placed him under the warmth of their wings to bring back the heat of life to his perished body, and Conn said:

'If only Aedh were here now, all would be happy with us.'

And after some time, indeed, they did see Aedh coming towards them and his condition very different from that of the other two for he swam proudly on the lip of the ocean, his head erect and his feathers dry and radiant. He was welcomed by the others and told them that he had succeeded in finding shelter in a Scottish cave from the fury of the storm. Finola placed him before her breast while the other two sheltered under her wings, and she said to them:

'Oh, it is wonderful to be together again. But we must be prepared for many more nights like this so let us not be either too disheartened or too optimistic.'

And so they lived for many lonely years on the Sea of Moyle. They suffered and they endured and they were bound together by their hardships and their love for one another, until one night of great wind and snow, storm and frost, so severe that nothing they had undergone before that or nothing they were to undergo after it could surpass it. The cold that was in that night might have come from the uttermost regions of the infinite sky, and the wind from the bowels of the turning earth; the frost fell and enveloped them like a covering of fire and the storm broke the sea asunder where they struggled to survive.

As the nights of that storm passed from one torment into another the very waters of the heaving sea became frozen into torn and ragged walls, grotesque and ugly all around them. They had reached Carricknarone in safety, but their feet and wings were frozen solid with the high flung spray, and manacled with ice to the torn floor that was the sea, so that the skin was ripped from their feet as they moved and the quills from their wings and the protecting feathers from their battered breasts.

When the salt of the sea reached their cuts and wounds their torture was doubled, and yet they could not leave the blasted Sea of Moyle for a safer retreat. They were forced to swim out into the channel where the water had not frozen, and, wounded and torn as they were, had no choice but to remain there in the sharp and bitter stream. They stayed as close to the coast as possible until the fearful cold passed and their feathers grew again on their breasts and wings.

Nothing again ever compared to that time, and for many years afterwards they lived close to the coast, now of Ireland and now of Scotland, but always they remained on the Sea of Moyle.

Then one day they were swimming by the mouth of the River Bann in the northern part of Ireland when looking towards the land they saw a great cavalcade of chiefs and lords riding from the south. They were mounted on white horses and as they approached the splendour of their cloaks blazed across the fields and their weapons glinted in the sunlight like the gathered stars glinting in the night.

'Who are these warriors,' asked Finola.

'I've no idea,' replied Fiachra, 'unless they are a party of Milesians, for they would hardly be our own people riding abroad in the land.'

'Let us swim closer to the shore and find out,' suggested Conn, and with that they swam together towards the River mouth where the horsemen were heading. They, in their turn, when they saw the swans coming towards them, changed course so as to meet them. They were indeed a party of the de Danaan led by the two sons of the Bodbh Dearg, Aedh and Fergus. They had been searching for the Children of Lir for many years before they found them, although they had traversed the coast of the Sea of Moyle backwards and forwards for so long that they knew every blade of grass on its margins and every pebble that lay on its beaches.

Now that they had found them they exchanged the warmest greetings of friendship and love and the Children of Lir at once asked about their father and the Bodbh Dearg and the others of the de Danaan whom they had known at Derravarragh and before that at Killaloe and at Sidhe Fionna.

'They are all well,' said Aedh and Fergus, 'and they and the hosts of the de Danaan are now celebrating the Feast of Gabhann with your father at Sidhe Fionna. Their happiness would be complete if only you were there with them to share in the festivities, for they have no idea what happened to you since you were forced to leave Derravarragh and come to the Sea of Moyle because of Aoife's evil.'

The four swans looked at each other and their eyes clouded with the memory of what they had been through.

'No tongue can tell you the suffering and torment we have gone though here,' they said, 'it is too much to remember. But perhaps you will carry this song home with you when you go?'

And, so that Lir and the Bodbh Dearg might know that

they were still alive in spite of everything, they made this song to be carried back to the Feast of Gabhann:

> 'Gladness and laughter and great rejoicing
> Fill eyes and hearts of our people at home –
> Checked by their inner thoughts still voicing
> Grief for us on the slow sea's loam.
>
> Bleak and cold the home we know.
> Our sodden down is thin and light,
> Yet we wore once – oh, long ago –
> Clothes that glittered in the night.
>
> Once, too, our lives were filled with laughter,
> As our brimming cups of gold,
> Now pain and sickness follow after;
> Lost, forgotten, in the cold.
>
> Our beds are rocks in wave-torn caves
> Our lullaby the washing sea;
> No voice to hear but the tongueless waves;
> No sound but the pitiless sea.'

After this the de Danaan and the Children of Lir said farewell to each other, for the four swans had to return to the flow of the Sea of Moyle. Sadly they drifted away from the shore, their graceful necks and heads turned back so that they could look to where their friends waved to them as they floated away. When they were out of sight the de Danaan returned to Sidhe Fionna where they told the chiefs what had happened and how the Children of Lir were. The Bodbh Dearg, having listened to what they said, answered them; for Lir was so moved that speech was beyond him.

'It is not in our power to help them,' said the Bodbh Dearg. 'But we are glad to know that they are still alive, and we know that in the end the enchantment will be broken and they will be free of their sufferings.'

Now the children of Lir, after they left the host of the Tuatha de Danaan, returned to the Sea of Moyle where they remained for many years more. Countless were the nights and the days that passed them by; the months and the seasons as the years of their imprisonment accumulated. But at last it came to a close, and they fulfilled their period of three hundred years on the Sea of Moyle.

And when the time was up, Finola looked at her brothers and said: 'We must leave this place, and go to the west.' Again they were being hurled by the power of Aoife's long-lived magic into the unknown, and together they made this song before they left Moyle:

> 'Three hundred years we've spent
> Suffering here without rest;
> Now we may leave this torn and rent
> Sea, and fly to the west.
>
> Out from the cold sea of the east,
> To the far storms we fly,
> Battering the west like a wild beast,
> To live in the tempest's eye.'

Then, when their farewell to Moyle was sung, the swans lifted themselves from its cold billows and turned westwards across the face of Ireland. High they flew, not seeing what happened beneath them and not looking for fear that the longing it might bring would break their hearts, until they saw the western sea beneath them, peopled and dotted with many islands near the shore of Ireland. They came down on the sea at Iris Domnann near Glora, and were little better off there than they were in the sea of Moyle; it was not so cold, but the storms were greater, so that their hardship was not the same, but was of equal intensity.

Now it happened that there was a young man called Aebhric living close to the shore in this place, who had a great tract of land running down to the sea. Here he would hunt and spend his time and cultivate certain crops – for the land in that part of the world is not rich and game is scarce, so that crops must be tended by people of noble families if they are to find a living. While he was here one day he saw the birds and overheard them singing their wonderful songs and making that music which Aoife had bestowed on them the ability to make when she placed her curse upon them. Like everyone else who heard their music he came under its spell and was entranced by it so that he wanted no other joy or pleasure in the world other than to listen to it, and so he came there every day for that purpose.

Gradually he made himself known to the swans and they to him and it came as a small surprise to him when he found that they could talk and converse as well as sing. In time he came to love them very much and they him, and they told him their whole story from beginning to end. And it is true, though it may not be an easy thing to believe, that it is to Aebhric and him alone that we owe thanks for knowing the story at all. For he it was who told his neighbours about the speaking swans and they told more, and many people would come from near and far to hear Aebhric telling the story; but he would not allow the people to meet the swans themselves for fear that some harm might befall them, in spite of the law that had been passed by the Bodbh Dearg six hundred years or so before. He it was who arranged their story as it is here and who told it abroad, so that it was passed on from one generation to the next and so on down through the passageway of the centuries until it reached us.

But that is enough about Aebhric. The swans, meanwhile, found their hardships renewed to such an extent that to describe their hardships on the western sea would be only to repeat again the story of what they endured on the Sea of Moyle. There was, however, one night of difference. On this particular night black frost so severe and so prolonged lacerated the face of the land and of the sea that the whole of it was frozen, as it were, into one mass of coldness, and the sea from Iris Domnann to Achill was frozen into a thick floor of ice and the snow came thick and solid in a blinding, masking blizzard from the north west. No other night of their centuries of torment was so desolate; never was their pain so great, never such an accumulation of suffering so that the three brothers were unable to stand the immensity of it any longer and made loud and bitter and pitiful complaints. Finola tried to console them, but she could not for her own condition was no better than theirs and, indeed, it seemed as if the end for them all was not very far away in the white, terrible storm of the night, and she herself began to lament with the others.

But then a strange, and awe-filled thing took place; in the

depths of her misery and lamentation, Finola felt a spirit mingling with her own that was strange and terrifying, but comforting and consoling too; greater than anything she had ever experienced of destitution or of happiness, it was indescribable, intangible, mighty, and yet inexplicable and full of wonder she stopped her wailing and listened to herself, or, more properly, to what was at once within her and without.

Then, when she was sure of what it was she wanted to say, she spoke to her brothers and asked them to stop their complaining for a moment until they heard her, and when they did so she said this to them.

'Brothers, there is Something here with us that I do not understand, for it is past my understanding and past yours and past the understanding of any mere man, but It is so great and awe-inspiring, so manifest of Love and of Goodness; of things so far beyond my comprehension, and yet for which my whole being strives, that I must believe in It for It is Truth. It is the Truth that has made the world, the earth with its fruits and the sea with its wonders; the heavens with their infinity. Put your trust in that Truth, brothers, and It will save us.'

'We will,' they said, 'and we do; for we feel It too.'

And that is how it happened, that at that hour when they were beyond any hope from within themselves or from without, they believed and the Lord of heaven who had not yet made Himself known to the people of Ireland, sent them help and protection; so that neither cold nor storm, hunger or want of any kind troubled them from that time on while they remained on the western Sea. And so they remained there until they had fulfilled their appointed time.

CHAPTER FOUR

Then Finola gathered her brothers around her and said: 'My beloved brothers our time on the western sea has come to an end and we can leave without let or hindrance; let us go now and pay our respects to our father at Sidhe Fionna and the people of the de Danaan.'

Of course her brothers agreed gladly and, lightly, they rose up from the surface of the sea, casting round once above the bay they were leaving without regrets, and turned eastwards with happiness in their hearts, flying swiftly until they reached Sidhe Fionna.

But when they got there nothing but sadness and desolation was before them. The great castle that had once dominated the surrounding plain, where they had spent their joyful youth, was broken and tumbled. The windows gaped emptily, and the mortar had fallen from between the buckling stones that had themselves fallen in pyramidical piles from the once proud walls. Nothing stirred save the wind. The halls were empty and ruined and overgrown with rank grass and weeds; the villages and houses that had flourished about the castle were gone completely with nothing left to show that they had ever been there. Nothing remained but the falling castle.

In horror and pity the four swans clustered together and gave three great cries of mourning and sorrow, and sang this lament in the place where they had been born:

> 'Gone are the noble and stately halls,
> Crumbled the pillars and tumbled the walls;
> Weeds and nettles, bent and blown,
> Grow where our pride was overthrown.
> Gone: All is gone!
>
> Silence fills this empty place
> But for the winds that round us trace
> Faint whispers of forgotten shades
> Bright with rich, gay cavalcades.
> Gone: All is gone!
>
> No warriors here, no men at arms,
> No tales of victory and alarms;
> Heroes, chieftains, great and brave
> Are still and mouldered in the grave.
> Gone: All is gone!'

The Children of Lir stayed that night in the ruins of their father's castle, and several times during the night they stirred and felt uneasy as old memories came out of the crumbling corridors to trouble them; and when this happened they made their sad, sweet music as an offering and a tribute to the past.

Early next morning they left the site of Sidhe Fionna behind them and flew back again to the only home they had left, the western sea, where they circled over Inis Gloire and settled on a small lake on the island. There they sang so sweetly that all the birds of the island, and of the mainland, and of any place that was known to birds, came and settled there beside the lakeside to hear them sing and make music so that from that day to this, and until the memory of it has faded from the mind of man, the little lake became known as the lake of the birds, so thickly were they crowded about it and on it and near it.

During the day the swans flew from one place to another, gratified in their freedom; now they would go to Iniskea – where the lonely crane has lived in isolation since the beginning of the world and will live there until the day of judgement – and now they would go to the island of Achill or elsewhere along the shores of the western sea, north or south as they fancied, but always they returned to the lake to spend the night.

And so they lived their lives until Saint Patrick came to Ireland bringing with him the knowledge of the true faith; and until one of his disciples in Ireland, Saint Caemhoch, came to Inis Gloire. That night the swans heard a strange sound coming across the island and reverberating over the waters around it, one that they never heard before. They were frightened at its strange, repetitive sound, and filled with terror and began to run wildly about thinking that it meant something dreadful for them. In fact it was only Caemhoch ringing his bell for matins. The three brothers were more afraid of the sound than Finola, who had always shown herself to be the wisest and most sensible of the four Children of Lir, and, having listened to it for a while she said:

'Don't you know what that sound is?'

And they said: 'No. We hear it, and are afraid of it, for we don't know what it is or what it might mean.'

Then Finola said: 'That is the sound that we have been waiting for, and the end of our suffering is near; that is the voice of the bell which is the sign that soon we will be free of Aoife's curse.'

And together they made this song:

'Hear the reverberant boom of the bell
Throbbing down the aisles of Time;
The metal voice we've waited to tell
The end is near of Aoife's crime.

Listen, oh swans, to the throbbing bell
Ringing across the shaded night;
Rung by the priest in his lonely cell,
Yet, for us, the voice of light.

That is the bell of the Lord of all
Repeating His faith across the world;
Be joyful, brothers, and hear the call,
For soon in His arms we'll be safely curled.'

When their song was over the four Children of Lir stayed in silence and listened to the tolling notes of the bell in the evening until it faded away altogether on a last lingering note. Then, as the sun faded too across the lake and silence came with the approaching night, they began to make the most beautiful music they had ever made in their long lives in praise of and in thanksgiving to the Almighty Creator of heaven and earth whose instrument was at hand for their deliverance.

Caemhoch heard their music from where he was and he listened in great wonder, for he had never heard anything on this earth so magnificent as the music coming out of the night in that lonely place. Gently he made his way towards the source of the music, but could see nothing for night had passed his own hurrying feet, and it was dark. Nevertheless he stayed close by listening to the music and giving thanks, for he realised that it was the Children of Lir, whom he had come to find, who were singing.

When morning dawned he saw the four white swans lingering in the water close to the shore, and he spoke to them and asked them if they were the Children of Lir.

They told him who they were, and Caemhoch replied:

'Praise be to God that I have found you, for that is why I came here, having searched the coast from south to north and back again until now, always looking for you. Come ashore now and trust me, for I will end your enchantment.'

And the Children of Lir were filled with immense and profound joy when they heard what Caemhoch said, and they walked ashore and placed themselves under his care. He told them that it would take time and preparation and that they must put themselves entirely in his charge before what they wanted could come about, but they trusted the gentle priest – for indeed, they could do nothing else, but even if they could they would have trusted him anyway, such was his kindness and understanding. He brought them to his little house and, sending for skilled workmen, had two chains of silver made one of which he put between Finola and Aedh and the other between Fiachra and Conn. And so they lived with him for some time, listening to what he told them day by day and telling him of all that had happened and of all that they knew to have happened, during the past thousand years and before. He taught them and instructed them in his beliefs and they were his delight and his joy and he loved them with a great love and tenderness; and the swans on their part were so happy with Caemhoch that the memory of their long years of misery and suffering became dim and caused them no distress.

Now the king who ruled Connacht at time – which was about twelve hundred years ago as anyone can establish if he takes the trouble to enquire – was Lairgnean Mac Colman and his queen was Deichthe the daughter of Finin of Munster – the same king and queen mentioned by Aoife when she put her spell on the Children of Lir so long before.

Now Deichthe was a proud and vain woman and, like many another in an exalted position, was gracious and kindly towards the rest of the world – so long as she was satisfied that she had and possessed all that was best in it for herself. But she could not abide to think that there might be a thing or an attribute with another that she did not have or possess herself; and if it was with or belong to someone she considered beneath her station – as she considered most people to be – then her torment was all the greater.

It so happened that the story of the four wonderful singing and talking swans reached the court of Connacht and so the ears of Deichthe. She heard their whole history not once but many times and was consumed with desire to own the swans for herself as a great and unique wonder. So she went to the king and asked him to get them from Caemhoch for her. But the king was reluctant to do anything of the kind, knowing that the Children of Lir were not birds or beasts to be bought or sold for the vainglory of any man or woman. But, of course, he didn't put his objections to his wife like that, he just said that he could not. But she was adamant, for now her pride was hurt as well as her vanity since Lairgnean had never refused her anything she asked before, and she told him that she would not stay another night in his palace unless he did what she wanted. She, being a high-spirited and selfish kind of a woman who had often made similar threats before, the king paid little attention to her this time, but she left that very hour and fled southwards towards her father's palace in Munster.

When Lairgnean discovered this he was very upset, for in spite of her faults he loved her greatly, and sent messengers after her to tell her that he would do as she wished; but they did not overtake her until she was at Killaloe, as it happened. However, she returned with the messengers to Lairgnean's palace and as soon as she arrived he made promises to her that he would send to Caemhoch for the swans. Straightaway he sent messengers to Caemhoch asking that he would send the swans to the queen, but, of course, Caemhoch refused to give them.

Lairgnean became very angry at this, for now his own pride was involved and he badly needed someone anyway on whom he could vent his anger, since he was extremely put out by Deichthe's behaviour, and of course it was not possible for him to be angry with her the way things were. Some say, as a matter of fact, that Deichthe was with child and that was the reason for her behaviour, but be that as it may, when Lairgnean got Caemhoch's answer he went off in a rage himself for the priest's house. When he arrived there he asked Caemhoch whether it was true that he had refused to give the swans to the queen.

'Indeed and I did,' said Caemhoch, 'for I have no power to give them any more than you have power to take them.'

When Lairgnean heard this he became even angrier than before and, going up to the swans, grabbed hold of the two silver chains.

'No power,' he shouted, 'I'll show you whether I have power or not, priest, for they are coming with me this minute. If I have no power in my own kingdom, then who has?'

And with that he took the chains, one in each hand, and began to pull the birds after him from the house, while Caemhoch followed in case they might be hurt by the king in his anger.

And it was at this time that a strange and wonderful thing happened. The king had gone only a very little distance to where his horse was being held by one of his attendants when, suddenly, the white feathery covering of the four swans began to fade and their shapes to alter before the eyes of all who were present and in the broad light of the summer's day. Slowly the four Children of Lir began to reassume human shape, but with what a difference. For, instead of the four, golden, bright, happy, delightful children who had been the pride and the great love of the Tuatha de Danaan so long ago, they carried with them the accumulation of their years. Finola was transformed into a bent, old and extremely wrinkled woman whose flesh was shrivelled on her bones so that she seemed to be but bones itself covered with an ancient skin. Only the eyes sunken deep in her head bore the brightness of youth about them still; and her three brothers were equally old, white-haired and wrinkled. When the king saw what had happened he was transfixed with terror and fright; and then, instantly and without speaking a word, he turned and left, while Ceamhoch reproached and denounched him bitterly. Meanwhile the Children of Lir, unable to stand for they were so feeble, called to Caemhoch, and said:

'Oh friend and priest, help us and baptise us now for there is not much time. You will be sorry, perhaps, when we die, but no more sorry than we will be to leave you; all we ask is that you bury us here, together, standing facing one another with our arms about each other as we have often stood when we were in the world.'

And if it seems a strange request to us today that they should be buried standing, remember that such was the old custom among the Gaelic and Celtic peoples of long ago. When they made this request, they sang this last song – and it is a strange thing that the beautiful music they had made when they were swans left them, and they sang with old, cracked voices; but their words were beautiful and made in unison:

> 'Come, oh priest, and stretch your hand
> Forth, over us here;
> Our long pain is over and
> Death is near.
>
> Dig a grave, oh dig it well,
> Deep and wide;
> Where we can hear the tolling bell
> Asleep inside.
>
> Lay us as we often lay,
> Four together;
> Held upright in the cold clay,
> Four together.
>
> Lay little Aedh before my face
> Those at hand;
> And about each place
> A loving hand.
>
> And so we'll sleep for evermore,
> Children of Lir.
> Come, priest, and shed your power,
> Death is here.'

This song took all but the last remnant of their strength and Caemhoch hurried to baptise them before they died; and even as he did they died under his hand. When they died Caemhoch was moved to look up and, strange and yet perhaps not so strange in this story, above him he saw a vision of four lovely children whose faces were radiant with immense joy. They gazed at him for a moment with great love and affection, and then, perhaps because his own eyes filled with tears as he looked, they faded from his sight and were gone when he wiped the tears from his face. But he was filled with gladness because of what he had seen, knowing that the children who had suffered so greatly on earth would suffer no more but live in infinite happiness; yet, even so, when he looked down at the poor, crumpled bodies at his feet, he was overcome with sadness, and wept.

Then Caemhoch had a deep, wide grave dug near his little church and in it the Children of Lir were buried as Finola had requested with Conn at her right hand and Fiachra at her left and Aedh standing before her face.

When this was done Caemhoch raised a burial mound above them and a tombstone with their names engraved upon it and performed their funeral rites and made a lament, of which this story is part.

And that is the story of the Fate of the Children of Lir.

Graine to Fionn

There is one
For sight of whom I'd gladly spare
All! All the shining, golden world
Though such a bargain be unfair.

Diarmuid and Graine

Cormac Mac Art was king of Ireland. That was about a hundred and fifty years before the coming of Patrick to Ireland which makes it a considerable time ago, but not a long time according to the way the world is judged, for Cormac was a good deal nearer to our own time than he was to, let's say, that of the Dagda or even of his son, the Bodbh Dearg; but that is a point that need not concern us greatly now as it has nothing much to do with the story except to give you some idea of when it happened. Cormac was not only king, he was a particularly good and enlightened king at a time when there was no great incentive for kings to be either. He was the son of Art the Lonely, and the grandson of Conn of the Hundred Battles and he was known particularly for his learning and wisdom which have come down to us in the form of a book – which if it had been better studied by those for whom it was intended might have averted much mischief in the world – a book called Teagusc-Ri, or Instructions for Kings. Indeed it might be profitably studied to-day by kings, and those who have replaced them, for it is available enough and no less applicable now than it was when it was written. Besides this book which was his own, Cormac filled the court with scribes and philosophers, lawgivers and lawmakers and had the records and laws of his kingdom collected and written down in a great work which he called the Psalter of Tara, where he had his magnificent court. And at Tara he established three schools; one for history and philosophy, one for law and one for military science, and it is with the third, or more properly with the reason for it, that our story begins.

In the time of Conn of the Hundred Battles, and even before him, there had been recruited and maintained by the king a regular standing army in Ireland called the Fianna. Each province supplied contingents, but the whole army was under the command of one general who had his permanent headquarters on the Hill of Allen close to Naas, where he kept seven battalions of the Fianna in constant readiness. At the time of Cormac Mac Art's kingship Fionn Mac Cumhal was general of the Fianna, as his father had been general before him... but it is not necessary to go into that or how Cumhal met his death at the Battle of Castleknock and at the hands of Gall Mac Morna, because it is a long, involved and, sometimes, puzzling story without much satisfaction in it and without any place at all in the story of Diarmuid and Graine.

Now Fionn was a man of mature years at the time of this story with a son, Oisin, and a grandson, Oscar, both of whom were already full members of the Fianna, having passed through the military college at Tara described above; for that was the purpose of Cormac's academy, to instruct young men and boys in the art and science of war in preparation for service as officers in the Fianna.

Fionn was a strong, powerful man, as indeed he needed to be to command the respect and leadership of the Fianna; to his friends he was openhearted and generous, to his enemies implacable. Now when he was a boy a strange thing happened to Fionn. A wonderful fish, the Salmon of Knowledge, was believed to inhabit the pool of Linn Fiach in the Boyne, and it was further believed that whoever first tasted this salmon would acquire the gifts of knowledge and divination; and, indeed, it was prophesied that a person named Fionn would be the first one to taste the salmon.

Now there was a certain old man, a poet and bard of no great merit and a bit loose in the head, by all accounts, called Fionn, who had his heart set on being the first one to taste the Salmon of Knowledge – and God knows he could have done with the bit of strengthening it would do his wits, I suppose.

At all events he settled down for himself on the banks of the pool of Linn Fiach and spent his days, and a large part of his nights too, fishing in the pool in the hope of catching the Salmon of Knowledge. Now at this time Fionn Mac Cumhal was only a boy, but he was a boy whose life was in continual danger and he was on the run from his enemies, the Clann Morna whose chief, Gall Mac Morna, had killed his father at the Battle of Castleknock. Consequently the young Fionn didn't care to use his own name overmuch as he wandered from place to place as to do so might relieve him of his head, to which he was attached, so to speak. So, in disguise and giving the name of Domhnach, he arrived one day at the camping place of Fionn the Poet who took him on as servant to tidy the place up and so on while he was fishing for the Salmon of Knowledge... and lo and behold if one day he didn't catch the self-same salmon after all. With less wisdom than he might have shown if he had tasted the salmon first, he gave the fish to 'Domhnach' to cook for him, warning him impressively on no account to taste it whatsoever. Cheerfully 'Domhnach' proceeded to cook the fish and soon it was doing to his satisfaction; a pleasant smell rose up from it, and together with the smell, a great blister on its side. Now 'Domhnach', who was a reasonably good cook, knew that the blister didn't mean a thing, but absentmindedly – for he was thinking about where he might go next once he got away from this silly old poet who spent his time fishing – he pressed his thumb against it and got burned. Promptly and with a yelp he stuck his thumb in his mouth and sucked it.

When the fish was cooked he brought it to Fionn the Poet on a platter and the old man sat down before it, clasped his hands and closed his eyes with a look of fatuous ecstasy on his face. Soon his patience would be rewarded. Gently he opened his eyes; reverently he picked up the fish in his hands – which he had even taken the trouble to wash beforehand – and bit into the flank of the salmon. He swallowed expectantly; and then waited a moment. But nothing happened. He blinked. Still nothing happened. He was just as stupid as before. Slowly he turned to 'Domhnach'. 'Did you,' he asked, 'taste the fish?'

'No,' replied the lad, 'but I burnt my finger on it and sucked it.'

'Ah,' said the old poet sadly, 'then you are no Domhnach. Your name is Fionn and in you the prophecy has been fulfilled.'

This is the story of how Fionn obtained his wisdom and power of divination, which were both great and accurate; but it is likely that it is no more than a story built up to account for the general's extraordinary perspicacity which, of course, is one of the reasons why he was a general.

In the course and fulness of time Fionn became the general over all the Fianna, even over the Clann Morna who were his enemies, and lived in his castle on the Hill of Allen. Now, although it was where his castle was, Fionn was under *geasa,* the most solemn vow which could not be broken without loss of all honour and reputation forever, which forbade him from sleeping there for more than nine nights in succession. One day he was sitting with the chief men of the seven battalions when one of them, Bran Beag O Buachan reminded him that this was the tenth day with the tenth night already beginning to encroach on it. Fionn looked up, startled.

'Indeed,' he said, 'I had forgotten. But where will I go tonight?'

He wasn't very worried as any of a hundred great houses in the vicinity would gladly have welcomed him, but he had accepted hospitality from all of them and he did not want to abuse it.

The restriction applied to no one but Fionn and most of the others moved off when they saw Fionn thinking, for they didn't particularly relish the idea of accompanying him to some strange house or other when they had the night in Allen well planned before them. Only a few stayed behind, and among them was Donn Mac Duibhne, and it was he who answered Fionn's question.

'Well,' said Donn, 'maybe we can have pleasure and entertainment for both of us to-night where you've never received it before.'

Fionn looked at him, because there weren't many houses he hadn't visited in the length and breadth of Ireland, but he said nothing and Donn went on.

'My son, Diarmuid, is fostered with Angus Og of the Tuatha de Danaan, at his palace at Brugh na Boinne. And, because of who I am' – said Donn swelling his chest a little, for he was a vain enough man, though it was his only foolishness – 'Angus's steward's son was fostered with him to be a playmate and companion, and the steward, being only a common man, agreed to send each day to the Brugh food and drink for nine men as the price for having his son fostered with mine. And so I am free to visit the palace of Angus when I please, together with eight companions, and claim the food sent by the steward – otherwise Angus's people get it. Furthermore,' he said, 'I haven't seen Diarmuid for more than a year, and we are sure to get a welcome.'

The idea appealed to Fionn, who wasn't too familiar with

the homes of the great de Danaan, and together with seven companions and their hounds they drove to Brugh na Boinne in their chariots. Angus welcomed them and had a banquet for them and brought in harpers and minstrels to pass the time while the food was being prepared. Diarmuid and the steward's son were there, two lovely children, darting about the place with laughter on their faces. Donn was as delighted to see his son as Diarmuid was to see his father and the great Fionn of whom he had only heard and with whom he some-day hoped to serve. But the visitors noticed that while Angus loved Diarmuid very clearly, equally clearly the people of his house favoured the steward's son. Donn disliked this, for his pride was offended that a steward's son should be favoured by anyone above his own, and he brooded on it until the hurt to his vanity brought a cloud on his mind. He sat silent and glowering throughout the banquet, but no one seemed to notice except Fionn who knew him very well. But he kept his counsel to himself and didn't ask Donn what troubled him for, being Fionn, he had noticed how things were too.

That night, after the banquet which was held in the great hall, the hounds began to fight over some scraps of meat that had been thrown to them, and there was great snarling and snapping and threshing of great bodies about the hall so that the women drew back in panic, and the servants fled. The two children didn't know whether to fly like the women and servants, or to stay and enjoy it like the men; and their hearts sprang into their great eyes as they looked at the fighting dogs which no one could, or would, separate. Whenever a dog came too near they would back away hurriedly, falling over some piece of furniture as they did so, while the dogs ravaged each other about the hall.

The eyes of all the men present were fastened on the fight, consequently they did not notice the son of the steward run between Donn's knees in the dimly lit hall. Remembering the favouritism the people of the house showed him above Diar-muid, Donn gave the lad a sudden squeeze and killed him on the spot. Then, in the confusion and without being seen by anyone, he threw the body under the feet of the hounds.

When, at last, the hounds were quietened, the little body was found and the steward nearly lost his reason at the sight. Everyone there tried to comfort him, but it was almost impossible. At last he turned to Fionn and said:

'Fionn, of all the men in this house to-night, I am the most harmed. The boy was my only child, and now he is killed by your hounds and I demand a suitable eric fine for him.'

Fionn said nothing for a moment. He was compassionate towards the man, but also anxious that justice be done, so he said:

'Examine the body of your son and if you find on it the mark of tooth or nail, then I will give you the eric you demand.'

So the body was examined, but no hurt, either bite or scratch, was found on it. The steward looked up wildly from where he crouched above the body of his son and his eyes glared at the assembled company. Then he turned on Fionn and cried:

'You, Fionn, have the power to uncover the hand that did this; yours is the wisdom and the divination of the Salmon of Knowledge and I put this *geasa*, this solemn vow, on you to identify the murderer of my son.'

Fionn had been afraid that something like this would happen. Whether the steward called on the so-called power he had from the Salmon of Knowledge, or whether he appealed to Fionn in his capacity as a wise and skilful man difficult to deceive, is of no importance. What is important is that Fionn accepted the geasa – indeed he had little choice, and brought to bear on the problem what he knew and what he divined in whatever manner. The conclusion he reached, of course, was the correct one, that Donn, in a fit of jealousy, had killed the steward's son. Not wishing to make this known, Fionn offered to pay any eric fine the man demanded, but he refused, saying that it was his right to know who killed his son. And so Fionn was forced to tell him. Then the steward said:

'It is easier for Donn to pay my eric than for any other man in this house, and the eric I demand is that his son, Diarmuid, will be placed between my knees; if he gets off safe, then I will forget the whole matter.'

When Angus heard this he rose up in anger and would have arrested the steward there and then; but Donn was even quicker and, drawing his sword, would have struck the head from the steward's shoulders if Fionn had not come between them and saved the steward. They stood like that for a moment, their hate electrifying the air between them, and then the steward turned and walked away. Coming back, silently, a moment later, he struck the body of his son with a golden druidical wand and transformed the dead boy into the semblance of a great, bristling, wild boar having neither ears nor tail.

Then, standing above the boar, with the wand in his hand, he made incantation:

'For this boar and your son Diarmuid, I decree the same lifespan; and when it is fulfilled, then they will kill each other. Then shall my son be avenged.'

And the moment he had said this the boar rushed out through the door and vanished into the night. The steward followed and neither of them were seen at Brugh na Boinne from that time onward. When he heard the terrible curse of the steward Angus, in his turn, placed a *geasa* on Diarmuid, who was still and silent at his foster-father's feet, and it was that during his entire lifetime he could hunt anything that he desired, save only a wild boar.

Now all this happened long before the story of Diarmuid – and it is the same Diarmuid – and Graine began, but it has an important part to play in it.

One morning, many years later, Fionn rose early and went out onto the slopes of the Hill of Allen before his castle. It was very still and quiet and the dawn was just a hint of light behind the horizon in the east. A blackbird sang somewhere alone – for blackbirds are always the first to sing in the morning – and Fionn looked about him as things began to distinguish themselves from the dark cloak of the night.

Two officers of the Fianna, Oisin his son, and Diorraing, son of Dobhar O Baiscne came round the hill towards him. They were on duty that night and were surprised to see Fionn abroad so early.

'What brings you out of your bed at this time of the morning?' asked Oisin.

Fionn looked at him sideways to see if they were baiting him, but they were not. 'Well, to tell you the truth,' he said, 'tis no pleasure to a man to spend the long morning in bed by himself.'

Oisin laughed. 'Tis little you have to trouble you,' he said, 'why don't you sleep while you can?'

'Who can sleep easy,' growled Fionn, 'when his life is lonely and he has no wife to comfort him?'

The others saw that he was serious, and grunted their agreement, whether they meant it or not.

'That's the way I've been this long time, unable to sleep or to rest since Maignes, daughter of Garad, died on me.'

'Well, of all the men in Ireland,' said his son, Oisin, 'you have smallest cause to complain. There isn't a woman in the country wouldn't give all she has, and more, to share your bed with you; and anyway there isn't a female, virgin or woman, in the green girdled island that we wouldn't bring you once your eye lit on her.'

'If it comes to that,' said Diorraing, 'I know a girl above all others in the country fitting to be your wife, this minute.'

'Who?' asked Fionn.

'Graine, daughter of Cormac, king of Ireland and son of Art, son of Conn Cead Cath. Of all the females I know, woman or girl, she's the most beautiful, most intelligent, most wonderful of the lot.'

And they knew that Diorraing didn't speak lightly when he said that, for he was the kind of man who would know about these things.

Fionn looked at him thoughtfully for a moment. He was impressed by what he heard – for he had not seen Graine himself since she was a small baby for reasons that will be clear in a minute – and the lonesomeness of his nights and private hours weighed on him heavily. Although he was a great commander and a great companion, he was also the kind of man to whom the love and attention of a woman was necessary; a woman with whom he could share the secret and gentler side of his nature that he sometimes thought of as the weaker side. It was a great hunger in him which he would have to satisfy one way or another, and it occured to him that if it was going to be satisfied at all then the finest available was worth seeking.

'There is a problem,' he said. 'King Cormac and myself haven't been on the best of terms for some time, and there is a little distance between us; if he were to refuse me in this there would be the width of the Shannon between us over it, and that wouldn't do. Let you two go to Tara and ask for me;

if Cormac refuses, well and good, no one need hear another word about it; but it would be better if he refused you than me.'

'Good enough,' said Oisin, 'but say nothing yourself about why or where we are gone unless we get a favourable answer.'

So, after they had eaten they prepared themselves for a visit to the king, had their chariots made ready and set off. When they arrived at Tara, Cormac, as it happened, was in council. Even so he welcomed the two officers of the Fianna and adjourned the meeting, for he was certain that two of Fionn's officers had come to see him on important matters. When they were alone Oisin and Diorraing told the king what their errand was. Then, in his turn, Cormac looked at them speculatively before replying.

'There is hardly,' he said, 'in all Ireland a prince or young noble who hasn't sought Graine's hand, and they have all been refused. But not by me. Yet each and every one of them holds me responsible for it, for she has always made me answer for her. This time, however, she must answer for herself, since I do not want the differences between Fionn Mac Cumhal and myself to widen as might happen were the refusal to come from me.'

Oisin and Diorraing were pleased to find that the king felt about the situation precisely as Fionn himself did, so when Cormac suggested that they ask Graine herself they agreed instantly. So Cormac brought them to the women's quarters in his palace, and into Graine's bower with its window of blue glass and he introduced Oisin and Diorraing and asked her to fetch them bread and meat and wine so that they might relax while they talked. And Oisin and Diorraing were very impressed at this treatment by the king, for they were, after all, merely officers in his army. But Graine said nothing but instructed one of her maidens in waiting to provide the food and drink. Then Cormac sat on the couch beside her and said:

'These two young officers are here on the instructions of Fionn Mac Cumhal to ask your hand on his behalf. What answer do you want to give, daughter?'

Now Graine, who was indeed a most beautiful woman, but perhaps a trifle spoiled and wayward, hardly looked at the two young men; and her answer was as languid and as evasive as her looks.

'I have no idea if he is a fitting son-in-law for the king of Ireland,' she said, 'but if he is, then why would he not be a fitting husband for the king of Ireland's daughter?'

This reply did not please Cormac, who was a man of straightforwardness and righteousness. Angrily he said:

'There are no ifs about it so far as I am concerned.' And he looked sternly at his daughter for a reply, but she did not answer.

The two emissaries said nothing to this, but secretly studied the princess, who, slightly flushed, looked through her window away from them, as she was somewhat put out by her father's rebuke. Diorraing noticed that she was wearing a coronet of gold about her head and an amber jewel about her neck, and – for he was a romantic young man – said to himself that, like the amber and the gold, Graine was a fine and rare woman, but unpredictable; while Oisin, the poet, was more practical and observant in his assessment of her. He noted what he could about her so that he could give Fionn an accurate account of her when he went back to Allen Castle. She was young, he thought, to be in the place of his own mother; indeed, she was younger than either of the two wives Fionn had had even when they were their youngest. On the other hand, she was lovely and she was accomplished. Her hands were long and well-shaped, and her finger-nails well-kept and reddened; she was long legged, from ankle to knee and from knee to thigh. Her hips were full and round, her waist slim and her stomach flat with beautiful, well shaped breasts filling two halves of her garment above. Her lips were red and not too full; her eyes were bright, but not sunken. Just as he was considering her eyes she turned and looked at him steadily, but like one who keeps her thoughts to herself.

'She would,' he thought, 'make a good wife for Fionn, for she is attractive, intelligent and displays the dignity of a princess.'

Cormac then suggested that Fionn himself should come to Tara in the following month when he would have prepared a banquet to welcome him and at which it could be announced that Graine and Fionn would be married, and her hand publicly be placed in his.

Then, for the first time for a while, Graine spoke.

'I have never seen Fionn,' she said, 'what does he look like.

Is he like either of you?'

'Indeed,' said Oisin smiling, 'if he is like either of us he should be like me, for I am his son.'

Graine looked at him with her steady gaze again, and Oisin felt suddenly embarrassed.

'Ah yes,' she said, 'Fionn would have a son who has reached an age when he is as famous as you are, Oisin.'

And Oisin, unaccountably, blushed again.

However, Oisin and Diorraing returned to Castle Allen in Leinster – for it should be noted that Ireland, at that time, was divided into five provinces, not four, and the fifth was that of Meath where Royal Tara lay. They reported to Fionn everything that had happened, how they had been well received by the king, how Graine looked and how the king had appointed a day for Fionn to come to Tara. And when the Fianna heard the news they gave three great shouts of joy that their general was to be married to the king's daughter.

And, as all things wear away, so the time between then and the coming of Fionn to Tara for his bride wore away and, with the officers of the seven battalions of the Fianna as a guard of honour, Fionn set off from Allen.

Cormac received them with great honour and ceremony in the great hall of Midcuartha where he sat on his throne on the raised, crescent-shaped, platform in the centre of the hall where he could be seen by everyone who was there, and that was a great number. He placed Fionn to his right, while on his left sat his queen, Eitche and on her left Graine and all the others were seated for the banquet that followed according to their rank and station.

As the banquet progressed the talk became centred in little groups here and there and Fionn's bard and druid, Duanach Mac Morna, who was sitting near Graine, sang and recited to her in a low voice many of the songs and poems and stories of her ancestors and their original kingdom, Cruachan, from where they had come to be the kings of Ireland at Tara.

After listening to him for a while, Graine asked:

'What brings Fionn to Tara to-night, Duanach?'

Startled, he answered: 'If you don't know, then it is hard for me to know.'

She was silent for a moment at this. And, perhaps, it should be pointed out here that there was nothing strange or odd in

Duanach's sitting beside Graine, for the Irish people of that time, in their great wisdom, ranked bards and lawmakers as equal with kings and nobles and treated them accordingly.

After a moment Graine spoke again.

'I'd like you to tell me what brought him,' she said.

'It's strange that you of all people should ask that,' said Duanach, 'for surely you know that he has come to ask for you as his wife?'

Graine was silent again. Then she said:

'If he had come to ask me for Oisin, his son, or Oscar itself, his grandson, then I could understand it and there would be nothing to wonder at. It would be more fitting for me to go to one of them than to a man who is older than my own father.'

Wisely Duanach said nothing. Graine was quiet again with her own thoughts for a while. Then she said:

'That is a great company of men who came with Fionn, but I don't know one among them except Oisin. Tell me, who is that warrior to his right?'

'That,' said Duanach, 'is Gall Mac Morna, the terrible in battle.'

'And the young man beside him?'

'Oscar, Oisin's son,' said Duanach.

'And who is that graceful man beside him?'

'That's Caoilte Mac Ronan, the swiftest runner in all Ireland.'

'And next to him, the proud and haughty looking one, who is he?'

'That,' said Duanach, 'is Fionn's nephew, Mac Lughaid.'

'And beside him, the one with the gentle, handsome face, and dark curls; he's speaking now, with a soft voice – who's he?'

'That,' said Duanach, 'is Diarmuid O Duibhne, beloved of all the Fianna for his nobleness, his bravery and his generosity – and not only by the Fianna,' he added with a smile, 'but by every maiden who ever saw him as well. The foster-son of Angus Og.'

'Indeed?' said Graine, 'that sets him apart from the rest of you, then, for it isn't every one is fostered by one of the Tuatha de Danaan. Who is that beside him?'

But Duanach had been asked a question by the king and

was busy answering it. Graine looked around until she caught the eye of one of her ladies-in-waiting. She beckoned to her.

'Get me my golden goblet – the jewelled one my father gave me on my birthday,' she said. 'It is in my jewel box.'

When the goblet was brought, Graine filled it to the brim – and that was no small measure, for it was a great, two-handled, jewel encrusted goblet, that no one man could empty at a sitting – and said:

'Take it now to Fionn from me, and say that I would like him to drink to me from my own goblet.'

When the lady-in-waiting gave Fionn the goblet he was pleased that Graine sent it to him first and, standing up he raised the goblet and took a draught from it before passing it on to King Cormac. Cormac gave it to his wife, the queen, who in turn passed it on and so it went about the lords and nobles sitting at the high table.

But Graine had put a powerful drug in the goblet and soon its effects were noticed for those at the table became drowsy and soon they had all fallen into a deep sleep; Fionn, the king and all those who had supped from it. Then Graine stood up from her place and went to where Diarmuid was sitting. With her heart beating in her breast and her eyes lowered, she spoke to him in a low voice.

'Diarmuid,' she said, her voice trembling, 'I love you.'

His head jerked as if he had been struck, and he looked, wide-eyed up into the earnest, shy, but determined face of the beautiful girl. Then his wonder changed to amazement and alarm as he thought of Fionn, his commander, and his duty. And although he had been filled with joy when he realised what she said, he answered her sternly.

'You are to marry Fionn,' he said, 'I cannot love you and even if I could I would not.'

'I am not yet married to him, Diarmuid,' she replied, 'will you return the love I give you?'

Even though they were speaking in low voices, the tension between them was electric and had communicated itself to those others in the great hall who had fallen silent now and were watching them. But they were unaware of it at the time.

'I cannot, Graine. You do not know me to begin with...'

'That is not so,' said Graine. 'I know you well. Do you remember a hurling match that was played between the men of Tara and the Fianna in which you saved the match for the Fianna by scoring two goals against my brother, Cairbre?'

'I do,' said Diarmuid.

'I watched it,' said Graine, 'not from the field, but from the window of my room. And I saw how you, when one of the Fianna, was hurt, leaped from the sideline and picked up his hurl all in one movement, and never stopped in your flight until you scored against the men of Tara, and repeated it again a moment later. In that moment, too, my heart went out to you and I gave you my love, Diarmuid, and I will never give it to anyone else no matter what comes or goes.'

Diarmuid remained silent, looking at her mutely; for he was torn between his duty and the love that rose in him for the princess beside him. But he could not speak of one or of the other.

'I know well,' said Graine, 'that it is not right for me to speak so boldly; but you know my position. Would you have me married to an old man – a man older than my father – when I love you? Please, save me from this, Diarmuid.'

Then, with a frown on his face, and deeply troubled, Diarmuid answered: 'It is a wonder you wouldn't love Fionn who, more than any man alive, deserves the love of women and the respect of men... and why should you single me out more than any other of the Fianna or the nobles of Tara, for of them all I am the least worthy of your love. But even if you were to love me, and I love you –' and he faltered, for he did and he knew it – 'and we were to be married, there is not a wilderness or a fortress in the whole of Ireland that would protect us from Fionn's anger and revenge.'

Graine looked at him for a moment without replying, and when she did answer him there was a smile playing about her lips.

'Oh Diarmuid,' she said, 'I know that you are speaking from your sense of duty and not from your heart, for my love for you is so great and so understanding that I already know of your love for me even though you will not admit it. But now I am putting you under the obligations of *geasa*, and bind you under the laws of our ancient religion to take me from this palace tonight and make me your wife before Fionn and the others waken.'

Diarmuid was in a torment of love and despair, but he

made a last effort to retrieve the situation.

'Even if I agreed to your *geasa,* Graine,' he said, 'how could we get away, for you know as well as I do that when Fionn sleeps at Tara he alone has the privilege of guarding the keys of the great gates to the fort, and without them we cannot leave.'

But she said: 'There is a wicket-gate leading from my apartments that we can use.'

'No,' replied Diarmuid, 'for it is another *geasa* on me that I may never enter or leave a king's palace except by the main gateway.

'Then,' said Graine angrily, 'come or stay as you please, but I am going in any event with or without you.' And, paying no attention to the hundreds of pairs of eyes that followed her, she turned and swept angrily out of the hall.

Then Diarmuid turned back to his companions and, with a sudden feeling of guilt, understood that they had seen and overheard the whole conversation, for they had that silent and embarrassed preoccupation with silence that people acquire in such circumstances.

Being the straightforward and honourable man that he was he decided to take the direct course so, turning to his close friend, Oisin who was also Fionn's son, he said:

'What should I do, Oisin, for Graine has laid heavy obligations on me?'

'What can you do,' replied Oisin, 'you are blameless in this matter, but you must keep your obligations or lose your honour, and no man of us here will hold you to blame for that. Go with Graine, but guard yourselves well against the vengeance of Fionn.'

Then Diarmuid asked Oscar, Oisin's son, who said:

'It is no man who does not honour his obligations; go with her.'

'And you Caoilte,' asked Diarmuid, 'what do you say?'

'I have a wife of my own,' said Caoilte, 'yet I would gladly give the world's wealth if it was me the princess had offered her love to.'

Last of all Diarmuid asked Diorraing, who said: 'Even though it would mean the end of you and I were to cry over your grave, go with Graine.'

And Diarmuid, still in doubt himself, said:

'And do you all feel the same way?' And all together they answered 'Yes.'

Then Diarmuid stood up and stretched his hands out to his friends with tears in his eyes and took farewell of them, for he knew that the end of his days with the Fianna had come, and that when he met them again it would mean trouble and war for them all. Then, without saying a word, he put on his armour and his helmet, took his shield, his sword and his spears and strode out of the hall.

He climbed the ramparts and looked out across the plain beyond. There below him in the moonlight stood Graine, waiting. When she saw him she called up to him.

'Are you coming, Diarmuid?'

'Oh Graine,' he said, 'I don't know what to do. The life facing us is not fitting for a king's daughter, and I don't know where we will be safe from Fionn.'

Then Graine, sad and gentle but as determined as ever, said: 'It makes no difference to me, Diarmuid. I will go alone if I have to, but I am not going back to marry that old man.'

'Then you will not go on alone,' said Diarmuid and, taking his spears in his hands, he put the butts on the ground and, grasping them near the heads, vaulted across the ramparts and landed lightly beside her.

As he regained his balance she moved towards him and put her arms around him. Without a word he folded her within his cloak and made no further effort to deny the love he felt for her. The harshness and coldness of his voice was gone, and he spoke gently and lovingly to her.

'I love you, Graine,' he said, 'more than it is possible for me to say. You are all that I ever thought of or dreamed of, and there is nothing that I ever thought of or dreamed of that isn't you or in you. May I be worthy of your love...' and then he stopped because he knew the words were pointless and heavy; too heavy to express what he felt, so he folded his cloak around her again and gave his spirit up to hers for a long moment. Then he said:

'Let us go, Graine, for the further we are from here when Fionn wakes in the morning the better.'

They hadn't gone very far when Graine stumbled and cried out that she couldn't keep up the pace that Diarmuid was setting.

'Diarmuid,' she cried, 'I can't go on like this.'

He stopped, a worried frown on his face. Death lay behind them in the night, he knew, and was closing in with every passing minute.

'Go back,' said Graine, 'to the stables and get a pair of horses and a good chariot. I'll wait here for you.'

And back he went to the stables, which lay outside the palace, and yoked a pair of strong horses to a speedy chariot; then he turned the other horses loose and drove back to where Graine was waiting for him. He lifted her into the chariot and they drove through the darkness, facing towards the west. The sun rose behind them, and Diarmuid drove the horses faster, and it was full and broad day-light when they reached the wide Shannon. There Diarmuid broke up the chariot and threw the pieces into deep water. He led one of the horses across the broad reaching river, and left the other to stray along the eastern bank. When he had that done, he turned to Graine and said:

'It will be easy for Fionn to follow us this far, for our tracks are plain enough. But from here on we must vanish if we are to be safe, therefore it is better to abandon the chariot.'

Then he lifted Graine onto his shoulder and carried her across the ford so carefully and gently that not so much as the sole of her foot or the hem of her dress became wet. Then they went on into the fastnesses of Connacht where there are many places, unknown and hidden, in which to seek refuge.

For a long time they went from place to place, always pursued by the trackers of Fionn, until at last they found themselves in a forest where Diarmuid built a small cabin of clay and wattles, and there they lived off the land for a while.

Meanwhile Fionn's rage when he awoke the following morning and discovered what had happened was terrible. Indeed his jealousy and rage were so great that for a while he was incapable of either speech or action. But when his brain and his consuming passion cooled, leaving behind an anger perhaps more deadly than either, he sent for men of the Clan Nephin, the most famous trackers in Ireland, and therefore in the world, and set them after Diarmuid and Graine.

Their task was simple until they reached the ford across the Shannon but, as Diarmuid had travelled both up and down the far bank and laid several false trails, they were unable to pick up the true one. When they reported back to Fionn he looked at them coldly and said:

'Pick up that trail again, and stick to it, or I will hang every man of you on both sides of the ford to mark the spot where you failed.'

There was no course open to them but to follow and re-follow every mark, every trail, no matter how fresh or how old it was. Finally, with many of the Fianna following, they hit on the correct trail and followed it towards the south west.

'Good,' said Fionn, 'I know now where they are heading.'

Now, as it happened, Oisin and some of Diarmuid's other friends were with Fionn when the men of Clan Nephin reported that they had picked up Diarmuid's trail again, and they were worried.

They discussed the position among themselves and Oisin, who knew how much Bran — one of Fionn's great hounds — loved Diarmuid as well, took the hound and set him on the trail ahead of the trackers. Without once losing the trail he followed it night and day until he eventually reached the place where Diarmuid and Graine were hidden in the depths of the forest. Silently he crept into the little cabin and placed his muzzle on the bed where they lay. Diarmuid started up, reaching for his sword, but Bran whined with pleasure and Diarmuid recognised him immediately. He also realised that he had come alone, for the first thing he did was to leap from the cabin and search outside, but there was neither sight nor sound of the Fianna to disturb the sleeping forest.

Graine was sitting up in alarm when he returned, afraid as much of the great hound that stood near her as of what Diarmuid might find outside. But when he came back he reassured her.

'It is nothing,' he said, 'only Fionn's hound which has been sent to warn us that he is close behind.'

'Then we must fly,' she said.

But Diarmuid would not leave. When Oscar and Oisin and Diarmuid's other friends came closer to the heart of the wood with the men of the Fianna, they found Bran returning, but with a drooping eye and dragging tail and Oisin was immediately alarmed. He suspected that Diarmuid had not taken the warning he had sent. So he spoke to Caoilte Mac Ronan who had a man called Fergor with the greatest shout of any man in the land.

'Tell Fergor to give a bellow out of him,' said Oisin to Caoilte, 'that Diarmuid might know how close we are.'

So with that Caoilte spoke to Fergor who drew enough air for six men into his lungs and let go a shout that rose the birds from the treetops, and the little animals from their nests in a pandemonium of fright, and which could be heard across half of the whole of Connacht.

And Diarmuid heard that shout. So did Graine – for she couldn't help it – and she said:

'What was that dreadful shout?'

'That,' said Diarmuid, 'is the shout of Fergor one of Caoilte Mac Ronan's men, and well I know it for I often heard it before and I think that they have him shouting now to warn us that he is near, and if he is near Caoilte and Oisin are near, for they are with him, and if they are near then Fionn and the Fianna are near for they are with the Fianna.'

'Then in God's name,' she said, 'let us go.'

But Diarmuid was very stubborn and very proud too when something like his honour was involved, but eventually Graine persuaded him to run with her from the pursuit of Fionn and he led her in safety through the forest.

When Fionn and the Fianna reached the place where they had been and found them gone his rage was terrible, and he let all who would see it; but he calmed himself in time, and finally decided to return to his castle at Allen and wait; for he felt that if he waited long enough they would fall into his hands at last. But nevertheless he made use of every opportunity to trap them.

He proclaimed Diarmuid as an outlaw and put penalties on any one who gave him any help or kindness. And so it was that, although Fionn had called off the Fianna, Diarmuid and Graine still travelled through the land as a hunted and wanted couple, living by the strength of Diarmuid's hand and the temper of his sword on the flesh of the wild deer and the crystal waters of the springs. As for Fionn Mac Cumhal, he had only one person in whom he confided, and she was his woman-spy and agent Deirdu, who went up and down the face of Ireland as this kind of a woman or that, seeking information about Diarmuid and Graine, where they sheltered, who were their friends and who were not; for it was – and still is very often — easier for an intelligent woman to glean this kind of information than it is for a man, as long as she's not too particular about how she does it.

Then one day as he was sitting playing chess with one of the chieftains of the Fianna in the sun-garden behind the castle, Deirdu slipped in through a wicket-gate that only she — beside himself — had a key to. She signalled to him from behind a shrub and he abruptly excused himself from the game and strolled away towards the end of the garden; he was by nature a secretive man who didn't like to let his left hand know what his right hand was doing, as the saying is and even though his battalion commander knew Deirdu quite well and the work she did, Fionn was more satisfied when he knew least, particularly when he knew less than himself. In a bushy arbour at the end of the garden he met Deirdu who was in the garb of a wandering druidess.

'Well,' he said.

'I have them located,' she said. 'They have fled to the fort of the ancients in the far west, the one known as Da Both. They are there now. I have asked Clann Morna to maintain a constant watch on them and track them if they leave... in your name,' she added hurriedly as he looked at her without change of expression.

And his expression did not change as his excitement mounted at her news. What he felt inside was not for her, or anyone, to share. But deep inside him, mounting his blood to his brain like the excitement of any passion flooding men from time immemorial, he felt the tide of anticipation rising in him hungrily. He knew the fort of which she spoke, it was one of the ancient, circular stone forts that had been dotted around the coastline for longer than the memories of man reached backwards into time. Built of high, loosely piled slabs of stone, the walls were anything from ten to twenty feet thick, often conical apartments contained within them, with access from the circular enclosure. Along the top of the wall there was usually a rampart with a small wall facing outwards, and, for a considerable distance around the entire fort there was a formidable barricade of closely packed, upright, boulders about three feet long, through which passage was slow and difficult. Only at the gateways to the fort was there a free passage. And it was here, in the stone huts and gloomy passages of the past, that Diarmuid and Graine had taken refuge. Fionn smiled to himself.

Then, taking with him several battalions of the Fianna, Fionn made a forced march across country, the infantry running beside the chariots and cavalry, until they reached Da Both, and as they went the foot soldiers hung to the chariots or saddles with one hand carrying their weapons in the other that they might travel more quickly.

When they reached the outskirt of the fort guarded by the Clann Morna, Fionn sent one of his trackers from the Clann Nephin to scout the position inside the fort and tell him who was there and how disposed. After some time the scout emerged from the night silently and said:

'Diarmuid is there,' he said, 'and a lady.'

'Is it Graine?' asked Fionn.

'I do not know,' replied the scout, 'for I never saw the lady Graine, but there is a lady within anyway.'

And then in a spasm of sudden rage Fionn swore at Diarmuid:

'Curse him,' he said, 'and bad luck to him and all his friends with him; he's here now but he won't leave here alive.'

Then he stood up in a rage facing the fort and shouted: 'Do you hear me O Duibhne; you won't leave this rat-hole of yours alive, do you hear?'

But there was no reply, nor any sound, from the great, silent, stone fort darker than the darkness ahead of them.

Then Oisin said, and his voice carried through the stillness of the silent army:

'It is your jealousy Fionn has you blinded. Do you think Diarmuid would wait here for you to kill him?'

But Fionn turned on him: 'No thanks to you, my son,' he said bitterly, 'if he did, for this time you have no hound to send ahead and no gillie to shout and warn him. He won't leave here until he's dead, I promise you.'

Then Oscar, Fionn's grandson said: 'But Fionn, knowing Diarmuid as you do, what makes you think he would be here waiting for you to kill him?'

To that Fionn smiled a cold smile. 'Knowing Diarmuid as I do,' he said, 'we shall see.' Then raising his voice he shouted:

'Tell me now, Diarmuid, who speaks the truth; Oisin and Oscar who say you have run, or who say you are inside?'

There was a pause. Then back from the solitary fort came the clear, proud answer:

'Your judgement was never faulty, Fionn; Graine and myself are here; but no one will enter without my permission.'

And the battalions of the Fianna, Fionn standing among them on a hillock, saw against the night Diarmuid standing on the ramparts of the fort. They saw him raise Graine beside him and they saw him give her three kisses on the mouth while Fionn stood there staring at them. When Fionn saw that the fire of his jealousy blossomed bigger than ever and roared in his heart and he cried: 'For that insult alone I'll have his head.'

He placed the men of the Fianna round the gateways of the fort, a company to each and there were seven gateways, and warned them: 'If Diarmuid tries to escape by this gate, capture him and hold him here for me. But do not harm the girl.'

Now while all this was taking place outside, an even stranger thing was happening inside the fort. For, as Diarmuid strode vigilantly from corner to corner of the position he had chosen to defend while Graine crouched below above a cooking fire, Angus Og – Diarmuid's foster-father – suddenly walked into the firelight. Whether he had come through the ring of armed men, or through the fence of standing stones, or through some mystic power of the de Danaans Diarmuid neither knew nor cared, but he was glad to see him.

Angus looked at him and said: 'What is it you have done, Diarmuid, that Fionn's anger is turned on you?'

Then Diarmuid told him from the beginning, how he was under geasa obligation of the gravest sort from Graine, and in peril of his life from Fionn. Angus stood looking at both of them for a long time. Then he said:

'I have the power to come in here, and I have the power to go also so that those outside will not see – or will not have any knowledge of – my coming and my going. Come now and I will take you with me, one on each side.'

But Diarmuid said: 'No. Take Graine. I will stay here for it would not be honourable to do otherwise and I am tired of forever running. However, I will leave this place, and if I am alive I will follow you to Brugh na Boinne. If I am killed send the princess to her father, and ask him to treat her neither better nor worse than before for having taken me as her husband.'

Then, in spite of her protests and tears, Diarmuid kissed Graine and told her to go with Angus Og. But she cried and lamented so much that he feared the men outside would hear her and guess what was happening. Then Angus said:

'Leave her to me Diarmuid.' He caught Graine from behind by the shoulders and tried to turn her round, but she would not turn, crying and fastening herself on Diarmuid's breast. Then Angus Og stood back and spoke sharply and penetratingly:

'Graine!' She looked up. He repeated her name, and again repeated it. Gradually her wailing ceased, though the tears still ran down her face, and her head lifted. She turned to look at him.

'Now listen to me Graine,' he said, 'and to nothing else. You are to be quiet. You are sleepy and you will rest and you will hear nothing but my voice...'

And so it was, for presently she stood there, very still and docile, the expression of sleep on her face but with her eyes open. Diarmuid remained silent and awed at this exhibition of the de Danaan power. Urgently Angus Og whispered to him:

'Diarmuid. Listen to me carefully. Say good bye to her now, kiss her, she is all right. But I must hurry. She will do whatever I tell her to. But we have little time. I must go as I came, for the guards may soon wake from the slumber I put them under. I will expect you at the Brugh.'

And with that he folded his cloak about Graine and seemed to vanish like a wraithe in the one movement. But looking over the wall Diarmuid could, to his surprise, see him walking unmolested past the rows of motionless guards at one of the gates; guards who, apparently, did not even see him.

Now, when Graine and Angus Og left him, Diarmuid checked his armour completely, went up to one of the seven gates around the fort and stood, tall and straight like a pillar, deep in thought for a while. Then he lifted his great spear, the Gae Dearg, and hammered on the door with the haft.

'Who's there,' he called.

'Oisin,' came the whisper, 'and Oscar and the Clann Baiscne. Come out to us and you will come to no harm.'

'I will not go out,' replied Diarmuid, 'until I find the gate that Fionn himself guards.'

And so it was at every gate – save two. At the second gate were Caoilte Mac Ronan and the Clann Ronan who swore to fight to death for Diarmuid, but he would not go for fear of bringing Fionn's wrath on them. At the third door it was Conan Maol and the Clann Morna who also offered him safety, but Diarmuid would not go; next Cuan and the men of Munster offered him his freedom, but Diarmuid would not endanger them, and it was the same at the next gate which was guarded by the Ulstermen. At the sixth gate Diarmuid called again to know who was guarding the other side.

'Clann Nephin,' came the reply, 'no friends of yours, Diarmuid; come out this door, O Duibhne, and you will be the mark for all our swords and spears.'

And Diarmuid replied: 'Dogs and sons of dogs. Your only ability is to smell a track like the rest of your kind. I will not go out to you for I would not dirty my weapons with your disgusting blood.'

And he went on to the seventh and last gate. 'Who guards this gate,' he cried as he hammered on it.

'Fionn Mac Cumhal,' came the answer, 'and members of his Clann and with them the Leinster Fianna. Come out to me, Diarmuid, till I carve your flesh from your bones.'

'Through this door I will come surely Fionn,' said Diarmuid.

Then Fionn brought his men close to the gate and spread them along the great wall on either side, for fear that Diarmuid would slip across if he brought all his men to the one spot; for Diarmuid was too good a soldier and Fionn too old a one not to know a trick to draw the enemy off to one spot and penetrate at another.

But Diarmuid's trick was not the trick that Fionn expected. When Fionn had posted his men along the wall from the gate they guarded, Diarmuid climbed to the parapet directly above the gate and, using his great spears, vaulted forth, out beyond the men below, and was already running before they had time to turn around. To those figures that rose up in his path he gave short shrift and no mercy, he cut them down as he ran without stopping, and left a trail of dead and dying strewn behind him on the path as he vanished into the night.

He did not stop running throughout the night until long after the sounds of pursuit had faded away. Then, during the day, he hid himself carefully, and so, after several days of cautious journeying, he eventually reached Brugh na Boinne and his foster-father.

When he stumbled in through the great gates of Angus's palace he made his way directly to the sun-garden where he knew he would find Graine; she looked up as he came through the wicket-gate into the garden and the very spark of life itself all but fled through her mouth with joy when she saw him come towards her.

And that night they stayed there with Angus, but next day they knew they had to be on their way again. Before they went Angus, tall and wise and majestic, changeless and long lived, said to them:

'My counsel is that you fly from this place and from every place in which you are known, and in your going here and going there never go into a tree that has but the one trunk, nor a cave with but the one opening; never stay on an island that has only one landing place. Do not eat where you have cooked; do not sleep where you have eaten, where you have slept do not eat in the morning.'

And with this advice Angus said goodbye to them, and they walked out of his palace into the hunting world.

CHAPTER TWO

After leaving Angus Og Diarmuid and Graine travelled west and south until they came to the River Laune near Killarney – then, as now, a good river for salmon, but known as the Rough Stream of the Champions – and they stayed beside it for a little while, and then went on to the plain beyond, between it and the Caragh River, called the Grey Bog of Findliath. One morning, while they were still journeying westwards, they met a stranger coming towards them. He was a man of enormous size, even in a land where big men were common, with a fine noble bearing about him and a long stride beneath him; but the arms and armour he carried, while complete, were ill-cared for and unused.

Diarmuid greeted him and asked him who he was.

'My name is Muadhan,' replied the other, 'and it would suit me well to be your servant.'

'If I took you on,' asked Diarmuid, 'what could you do for me that I could not do for myself?'

'I will serve you by day,' said Muadhan, 'and watch for you by night,' which was a good answer since Diarmuid was for a long time feeling the ill-effects of too little sleep and too much concern.

So they made an agreement between them and Muahdan went westward with his new master and mistress. They reached the Caragh River and Muadhan proved his worth by carrying Diarmuid and Graine across it without bothering with a ford; once across they travelled on until they came to the River Behy and there they found a small cave on the side of a hill called Currach-Cinn-Adhmaid and above the sea where the Tonn Toma roars in wintertime with the forecast of rain.

Muadhan made the cave comfortable with rushes and birch tops for Diarmuid and Graine, and when he had that done he went out and cut, with a great, rusty knife that he wore in his belt, a long, straight branch from a mountain ash or rowan tree. Then he produced a line of hair from his pouch and a hook of bone, and fitting one of the red rowan berries to the hook he made three casts with the rod across the stream and with each cast hooked a salmon. Then he put by the rod until the following day. He cooked the fish, giving the largest one to Diarmuid another to Graine, keeping the smallest one for himself, and then settled himself at the mouth of the cave to keep watch while Diarmuid and Graine slept within.

Next morning as dawn came rising above the three humps of Currach-Cinn-Adhmaid, Diarmuid strode out upon the biggest of them, telling Graine to keep watch while Muadhan slept. From the top of the hill he began to survey the surrounding countryside and the sea to the west of him and it wasn't very long before he saw a small fleet of black ships making their way up the bay beneath. At the very foot of the hill where Diarmuid stood the ships turned for shore and more than eighty warriors disembarked from them. Diarmuid watched them for a little while, and then, with great leaps and bounds on his heels he hurtled down the hillside towards them.

When he reached them he greeted them and they, who had seen him coming and had stopped whatever they were doing until he reached them, returned his greeting. They were wild, hard-looking, ruthless sea pirates and Diarmuid didn't care for them at all.

'We are the three chiefs of the Ichtian Sea,' they said, 'Dubhcos, Fionncos, and Trencos. Who are you?'

Diarmuid looked at them for a moment. He had heard of these three, Blackfoot, Whitefoot and Strongfoot, and what he had heard didn't make him any happier to see them there.

'A man of the locality,' he said. 'What brings ye here?'

They looked sharply at him with their hard eyes. But he didn't move. 'We're here,' said one of them at length, 'at the request of Fionn Mac Cumhal who can't keep strange cocks out of his own nest,' and they all laughed coarsely.

Diarmuid smiled politely.

'So they tell me,' he said. 'What does he want you to do?'

'To pluck a cockerel for him.' They laughed again at this sally from Trencos. 'This Diarmuid O Duibhne is loose hereabouts it seems and Fionn, for all his Fianna, hasn't been able to get his hands on him... but what can you expect from a crowd like that anyway, soldiers...' and he grunted in contempt.

At this insult to the Fianna Diarmuid was tempted to draw his sword there and then and teach the foreigners just what the Fianna could do, but instead he smiled politely again, and said nothing.

'Fionn is paying us well to watch the coast while he combs the land behind so that we'll catch this outlaw between us,' said Dubhcos.

'And will you be able for him?' asked Diarmuid innocently.

'There isn't a man alive we're not able for,' said Dubhcos looking as black as the foot he was named after.

'And anyway,' said Fionncos, looking just as black in spite of his name, 'we have three man-killing hounds from Gaul that will track him down and kill him. Now, tell us, have you heard anything of him?'

'Aren't ye the lucky men ye met me,' said Diarmuid still playing the simple innocent, 'indeed I did see him and only yesterday. And it would be as well for you to pay attention to what I say and go after him with caution for 'tis no common man ye have to deal with when ye're dealing with Diarmuid.'

After some more of this 'innocent' talk, when, despite their bluster, he could see that he had them uneasy if not worried, he asked them if they had any wine on board as he was thirsty. Confident that they had found a mine of information, and since Fionn was paying them well with a bonus guaranteed if they took Diarmuid, the pirates said that they had and produced a barrel.

They all drank until the barrel was empty, and then Diarmuid said:

'Now I'll show you a feat that Diarmuid taught me so that you may know the kind of man you'll have to meet if you have the bad luck to catch up with him; and I'll challenge anyone of ye to perform it after me.'

Now Diarmuid wasn't as foolish in this as it might seem for, while his companions had dipped liberally into the barrel of wine and transferred its contents from there to their stomachs with great enthusiasm, he had disposed of most of the wine given to him in quite another way; he had spilled it behind him, or beside him, or before him or wherever happened to be handiest, but very little of it had gone inside him. So that he was now as sober as he ever was, while they were boastful and unsteady on their feet.

Diarmuid picked up the barrel and ran with it to the edge of a high cliff overlooking the bay. At the top the cliff was very high and it plunged down to the sea and the rocks below, but it tapered down towards the beach in a gentle slope, becoming less and less, so that if you walked along the top of it you would eventually reach the beach. Diarmuid placed the barrel at the highest part with half of it hanging over the cliff and then leaped up on it. It started to roll towards the beach with Diarmuid balanced on it hanging over the precipice, but he brought it safely down to the beach. Three times he did this with the pirates looking at him.

'You call that a feat,' they cried derisively, 'surely you never saw a real feat in your life.'

Then one of them laughing picked up the barrel and ran with it to the top of the cliff intending to repeat Diarmuid's trick. He put it on the edge of the cliff and leaped on it. As he did so Diarmuid gave it a push with his foot to set it going and the man immediately lost his balance and, with a terrible scream, fell over the cliff and was dashed to pieces on the sharp edges and points of the rocks below.

Then another one of them tried, and he too was killed in the same manner, and then another tried and then another and the upshot of it was that ten or eleven of them were killed before they would acknowledge themselves beaten and then it was only because Dubhcos ordered them to stop. So the others went back on board their ship, gloomy and muttering to themselves, very sober again.

Cheerfully Diarmuid left them and returned to the cave, and Graine was overjoyed to see him. Muadhan went then with his rod and putting another rowan berry on the hook, caught three more salmon as he had done on the previous night. He cooked them and shared them as he had done before, and then kept watch throughout the night while Diarmuid and Graine slept until the dawn flooded the mountainside again.

Then Diarmuid left the cave again telling Graine to keep watch while Muadhan slept, and he went back to the camp of the pirates where he found the three chiefs and their men on the shore before him. He greeted them and asked them if they would like to see any more feats of Diarmuid's:

'We'd much prefer to get some information about him,' they said surlily.

'Information is it?' asked Diarmuid innocently and wide-eyed. 'Well aren't ye the lucky men ye met me, and sure isn't that why I came here this morning, to tell ye the information I have?' He paused, and dropped his voice. 'I met a man who saw him this very morning, eating a fish by the side of a stream above...' and he waved his hand generously in the direction of the mountain. The three men made a start as if to set out after him there and then, but Diarmuid went on... 'Of course that's several hours ago and he'd be long gone since, but maybe 'tis no harm, for if ye met him when ye were unprepared it might go hard with ye. I'll show ye an-other feat of his now that he taught me that ye might know what to expect from him.'

And so saying Diarmuid took off his helmet and his

armour; his cloak and his tunic until only his shirt remained across his broad shoulders. Then taking the Gae Buidhe, his smaller spear, the one that had been Mananaan Mac Lir's, who had lived in Scotland in Amhain Abhlach, he fixed it firmly in the ground with the point upwards. Then, walking backwards a little, he ran towards it and with a leap, landed softly on the point, before leaping safely to the ground without wound or hurt of any kind. The onlookers were amazed that he had not been pierced and believed it to be a trick – which it was; and that he wore some protection in his shoe – which he did not. The matter lay in the head of the spear which could be adjusted by one who knew how. But the pirates did not know how.

One of them a dark faced surly fellow, stood up and said: 'If you call that a feat it is plain you have never seen one in your life.' And running towards the spear he made a great leap in the air and came down on the spear and was impaled through his leg as far as his heart so that they had a terrible job to retrieve the spear from inside him. Diarmuid repeated the feat; and then Diarmuid repeated the feat again. Several more men of the pirates attempted it, and all were killed, but they did not give up trying it until ten or twelve of them lay bloody and dead about the place and Fionncos ordered them to stop. After that they returned to their ships and Diarmuid, in great good humour, returned to the cave where Graine greeted him and Muadhan caught the salmon as before. After their meal Diarmuid and Graine lay down to sleep and Muadhan spent the night on watch.

Next morning Diarmuid went out on the mountain and cut two, strong forked poles which he took with him to the beach where the pirates were as before.

Diarmuid greeted them and after some exchange of conversation they asked him what the poles were for.

'I brought these,' said Diarmuid, 'to show you one of the feats of this O Duibhne that ye hunt.'

He then fixed the poles firmly in the earth and taking his sword, the Moralltach or Great Fury, that he had received from Angus Og himself, he laid it between the two forks with the edge uppermost and bound it in position with strong thongs. Then, with a light jump, he landed on the edge and walked gently three times from one end to another along the blade and then leaped to the ground without any sign of injury. He challenged the strangers to do the same thing.

Then one of them rose up with a black look and, not saying anything, leaped upwards onto the blade. But he fell heavily on it so that it cut him in two. Another tried the same and was killed also and they did not cease until as many were killed as had been killed on the previous two days.

They stopped at length only when Trencos ordered them to do so and were about to return to their ships when they asked Diarmuid if he had any news of himself.

'I saw him to-day,' he replied, 'and I'll tell you what I'll do. I'll go and see if I can find him and bring him to you in the morning.'

They were pleased enough at that, for they had begun to be suspicious of him – and not before their time, I suppose – and Diarmuid returned to the cave on the hill where the night was spent as before.

Next morning Diarmuid went out on the mountain and this time prepared himself for battle. He put on his great armour, which was of the strongest sort so that it was all but impossible to wound him anywhere. He hung the Moralltach at his left hip and took his two spears, the Gae Buidhe, or small spear of Mananaan, and the Gae Dearg or Great Red Spear, from whose wounds no one ever recovered.

Then he woke Graine and told her to keep watch until nightfall while Muadhan slept. When she saw him prepared for battle she was frightened and asked him what he intended to do.

'Have Fionn's soldiers found us?' she cried in alarm.

But he calmed her and told her: 'It is better to be prepared in case the enemy does come my way, but there is no danger.'

His calm words reassured her and he went down the hill to meet the foreigners as before. They greeted him and asked him if he had seen himself, and Diarmuid replied.

'He is not very far away, for I have seen him just now.'

At this they became very excited and demanded that he lead them to his hiding place. But he retreated a few steps from them and held up his hand as they rushed about to arm themselves, and they stopped what they were doing in their surprise.

'That,' he said, 'would be a poor way of repaying a friendship, and Diarmuid O Duibhne is my friend if he is anybody's and is now under the protection of my arms and armour, so you may be certain I will do him no treachery.'

When they heard this their rage was enormous and they cursed and swore at him. One of them said:

'Then if you are his friend you are Fionn's enemy and ours too; and now we'll have your head to bring him as well as that of Diarmuid.'

'Indeed,' said Diarmuid, 'that is a thing you might do if you had me tied hand and foot, perhaps; but since I'm not I'll make it hard for you.'

And so saying he drew the Moralltach from its scabbard and, as they drew forward to close with him, he sprang at them and clove the body of the foremost in two with one blow. Then he rushed through them and round them, seemingly above them and below them, like a wolf among sheep or a hawk among sparrows, cleaving them and slaughtering them until only a few were left who were hardly able to reach their ships and safety from his terrible fury.

After this Diarmuid returned to the cave and he and Graine ate and slept as before while Muadhan kept watch until the morning. Then, arming himself fully again, and taking his great shield with him, he went and stood on the hillside and struck his shield with his spear as a challenge until the sound of it echoed and rechoed across the bay and back from the surrounding hills. When he heard it Dubhcos immediately armed himself and sprang ashore to meet the challenger before the sound of the challenge had died away.

Now Diarmuid, after the insults and belittling of Dubhcos, had no wish to kill him quickly, and had a worse punishment in mind for him. So, casting aside his weapons, he closed with his foe and they struggled and fought until their muscles and sinews, their bones and veins strained and cracked with the agony; the earth seemed to tremble as they stamped under their raging feet and the very rocks threw back the noise of the combat. And so it went on until Diarmuid, with one immense heave, threw Dubhcos helpless to the ground and instantly leaped on him and bound him with chain-bound thongs. After Dubhcos came Fionncos and then Trencos and Diarmuid defeated each of them and tied them up in the same manner.

Now this is the way in which he tied them. He tied their feet together and he tied their hands behind their backs. Then he made a noose in the thongs and put it around their necks and he tied the running end of this about their feet which he doubled up into the small of their backs. Then, if they did not stretch their legs they became cramped and died of contortion, and if they stretched their legs they choked themselves to death. Leaving them writhing in pain on the ground, he said: 'I would strike off your heads, but that I wish you to die slowly and in torment; and die you will, for none can release you from these bonds until you die.'

Then Diarmuid went back to the cave and told Graine all that had happened and how he had caused nearly forty of the pirates to be killed in his feats and had killed many more of them in battle so that they were reduced to less than half their number. He told her that he had beaten and tied the three leaders and left them on the hill to die:

'Because,' he said, 'I want their torment to be long and not short. There are only four men in Ireland who can loosen them, Oisin, Oscar, Mac Lugha and Conan Maol, and I doubt if any of them will do it. Fionn will hear what happened to them and the news will sting him. But he will know we are here, so we must leave. Also the remainder of the pirates will set their man-hunting dogs after us, so we had better leave quickly.'

So they left the cave and travelled eastwards until they came to the Grey Bog of Findliath and whenever Graine was tired or they had to cross water or rough places Muadhan picked her up and tenderly carried her without sign of tiredness himself.

Meanwhile those of the pirates who were left alive had come to where their three chiefs lay bound and tried to release them, but the more they tried to undo the Persian knots that Diarmuid had put on them, the tighter they became. While they were doing this they saw Deirdu, Fionn's secret agent, coming towards them across the mountainside. When she saw the numerous bodies around she asked who it was had made the fearful slaughter.

'Tell us first,' they replied angrily, 'who you are for we trust no one after what happened here.' And they put the point of a sword to her throat and would have run her through there and then if she had not said:

'I am Deirdru of the Black Mountain, the agent of Fionn Mac Cumhal who sent me here to look for you.'

They relaxed then and told her what had happened. 'We do not know his name,' they said, 'but we can describe him. He was tall and with a strong face and jet-black curly hair beneath his helmet. He has been three days fighting and killing us, but what is worse is the condition in which he has left our three chiefs who will die unless we can untie them, and so far we have been unable.'

Then Deirdru looked pityingly at them. 'You poor fools,' she said, 'you have begun your quest badly for that was Diarmuid himself that was here.'

And they swore and cursed in their rage at the way they had been tricked and immediately brought out the three man-hunting dogs to track him and tear him down. Deirdru in the meantime said that she would return and tell Fionn all that had happened.

The three dogs picked up Diarmuid's scent immediately and led the blood-seeking pirates to the cave where they found the rushy bed that Diarmuid and Graine had slept in. From there they went eastwards on the track of Diarmuid and Graine and Muadhan until they came to the slopes of Slieve Lougher near Castle-island, where they had taken refuge.

As Diarmuid sat by a stream on the mountainside he heard the baying of the dogs and the shouts of the pirates coming towards him in the distance. He stood up and looked back and saw them making their way upwards and in front were three men in green cloaks with the slavering dogs held on chains. And when Diarmuid saw this he was filled with hatred and loathing and a terrible rage.

Muadhan lifted Graine and walked with Diarmuid a mile or so along the stream, but they were seen from behind and one of the green-cloaked warriors loosed the dog he held which came bounding towards them. When Graine heard his awful baying behind her she was terrified, but Muadhan bade her not to be frightened for he would deal with the hound. He drew from his belt a small sgian, or knife, and when the great hound, sleek and black with red eyes and venomous jaws came leaping at them, he threw the knife down the dog's throat and it fell at their feet dead and bleeding. Then

Muadhan extracted his knife and put it back in his belt again and they went forward once more.

Then the second hound was released from behind and they could hear it covering the distance between them and the pirates with great raging leaps, and Diarmuid said:

'I will try the Gae Dearg on this hound, for nothing can withstand it.'

And he turned while Muadhan and Graine went forward again. Diarmuid waited until the hound leaped onto a bank above him and then, putting his finger into the corded loop of the spear, he cast it with all his force at the beast, driving the spearhead down his throat so that his entrails were scattered about the mountainside. Then, leaping forward he drew the spear and followed Muadhan and Graine.

Soon after they heard the third hound close behind them and Graine looking back gave a cry of fright for this was the largest and fiercest of the three and he was closer than either of the others and had come on them unprepared, for he had travelled silently.

'Diarmuid,' she screamed, 'Diarmuid!'

Even as she screamed the hound sprang, at a place known as Dubhan's Pillar. But Diarmuid, sweeping Graine aside with one hand, ducked beneath the hound as he sprang to seize her, and grasped him by the two hind legs as he passed. He swung the brute around under its own momentum and flung it against the pillar, dashing out it's brains.

Then, fitting his finger again in the silken loop of the Gae Dearg which he had rewound, he threw the spear at the foremost of the greenclad pirates, and slew him. He threw the Gae Buidhe at the second one, and killed him also and then, drawing the Moralltach he sprang at the third and swept off his head. When the foreigners saw their leaders killed they turned and fled in complete disorder, while Diarmuid flung himself at them from behind killing and slaughtering them as they fled in panic so that there seemed no escape from him unless, indeed, they could fly above the trees like the wildfowl of the air, or hide themselves in the ground like the badgers and wolves or dive beneath the water if there had been any to dive beneath.

Meanwhile Deirdru had told Fionn that the pirates were on Diarmuid's track and, with the battalions of the Fianna, he set out at once for the hill where the three chiefs were lying. When he reached it they were nearly gone, crippled with the pain of their position, and he was angry and upset to see them like this. He knew that only Oscar or Oisin, Mac Lugha or Conan Maol could undo the fetters that Diarmuid had bound these men with, so he asked Oisin to loosen them.

'That I cannot do,' said Oisin, 'for Diarmuid put me under *geasa* never to untie an enemy that he bound.'

Next Fionn asked Oscar, but Oscar also refused saying that he would never undo an enemy of Diarmuid's; and when he asked Mac Lugha and Conan Maol they said the same thing.

At that moment the remnants of those pirates who had followed Diarmuid came running back from the field of battle, and there were few indeed of them, and they told what had happened there. And when the three chiefs heard this, being worn out with torment and suffering, they died of grief that their entire company save for these few were lost. Then Fionn buried them in one wide grave, placed a monument with their names engraved on it above them, and full of grief and bitterness, marched back to Allen with his battalions.

CHAPTER THREE

After all this Diarmuid and Graine travelled eastwards and northwards until they reached Limerick, and here Muadhan bade them farewell and left them, and they were sad when he had gone for he was very gentle and had served them faithfully, but he had to go his own way, and they understood that. So, on the same day that he left, they too left and turned their steps northwards again and didn't rest until they reached Tireragh in Sligo, which was at that time guarded by one Searbhan, a great Fomorian, who had been put there by the Tuatha de Danaan for a purpose. And the purpose was this.

Many years before a game of hurling had taken place between the men of Ireland and the Tuatha de Danaan on the plain beside Loch Lein in Killarney. They played for three days and for three nights without either side being able to win a single goal from the other during the whole of that time. And when the de Danaan found that they could not beat the men of Ireland, they were very put out and suddenly decided to withdraw from the game altogether – which wasn't very sporting of them – and they left the lakeside and journeyed northwards in a body.

Now the de Danaans are not like ordinary mortals as everybody knows, and they had brought for their food during the game and for the journey to and from Killarney, crimson nuts and arbutus apples and the scarlet berries of the rowan tree, which they had brought with them from Tir Tairrngire, the Land of Promise which, as has been said before, those who don't know any better call Tir na nOg. And, since these fruits and nuts had many secret virtues, the de Danaan were particularly careful that none of them should fall into the hands of the men of Ireland, or onto the soil of the land where they might grow. But as they passed through Tireragh one of the scarlet rowan berries dropped on the earth as they passed and they never noticed it falling.

From this berry a rowan tree grew and it had all the virtues of the trees that grow in Tir Tairrngire. Its berries had the taste of honey and gave anyone who tasted them a feeling of immense well-being, and if he was even a hundred years old, a man would return to the age of thirty when he had eaten three of them.

Now when the de Danaan learned what had happened they were alarmed in case anyone who wasn't one of themselves would eat the berries, and they sent a great Fomorian, this Searbhan, to guard the tree so that no one would approach it. He was a giant, as they say, of the race of Cain, huge and strong, and he carried an iron club tied by a chain to a massive belt that he wore around his waist, and there was no way of killing him except by giving him three blows of his own club. By day he sat at the foot of the tree watching for anyone who might come near, and by night he slept in a hut he had made for himself high in its branches.

Diarmuid knew all about Searbhan and calculated that he would be safe from Fionn and the Fianna in Tireragh, because Searbhan would not allow them to hunt there and neither they, nor indeed anyone else, would go within a dozen miles of the wood where the rowan tree stood for fear of the gigantic Fomorian, so that the land for miles around was a wilderness and a sanctuary for all sorts of game.

Leaving Graine safely in a dry cave, Diarmuid went forward boldly to where the huge Searbhan sat glowering at the foot of his tree, and told him that he wanted to live in the district and hunt the game and fish the streams there for food.

The great, surly, skin-clad guard turned his shaggy head and looked at Diarmuid out of the single, baleful, red-tinged eye he possessed; for he had lost the other one in some careless way or another in a fight in his youth. By god, thought Diarmuid, thanks be that he's not grown older than thirty from eating the rowan berries, for if he's that ugly at thirty, what unapproachable kind of an ugliness would he have at forty or fifty or more?

While Diarmuid was thinking this, the big man was studying him silently; then, in the few words of a man unused to much talk — easy to see he's a foreigner, thought Diarmuid — and in a voice as ugly as his appearance, Searbhan told Diarmuid that he could live where he pleased and hunt what he liked as long as he didn't try to steal any of the rowan berries, because if he made the attempt, it would be the last he would ever make.

And having said that much he said no more but glared unblinkingly at Diarmuid without moving his head or anything else until the latter went away out of sight altogether. Then the giant went back to his dozing again.

So Diarmuid built a substantial hut near a spring and put a strong fence all round it with only one doorway through it, and he and Graine lived in peace for a while.

Meanwhile Fionn had returned to Allen and to his castle and the Fianna to its normal duties and everyone thought that the fire of Fionn's anger against Diarmuid and Graine had died down; but this was not so. For, though he appeared to have mellowed in many ways on the surface, inside he was still a turmoil of bitter jealousy waiting its revenge. And one day an opportunity presented itself to him which he could not let pass.

While he was with some of the garrison troops on the great green before the castle, they saw a body of about fifty horsemen approaching from the west led by two who were taller and prouder looking than the others. They rode up at a fast trot and dismounted in front of Fionn, whom they saluted. He asked them who they were and where they were from, and was surprised and thoughtful at their reply, which was:

'We are your enemies, Fionn,' they said, 'but we are anxious to make peace between us. We are Angus and Aedh, the sons of the Mac Morna who fought against your father at the battle of Castleknock, when your father was slain, and for which you afterwards slew our father and outlawed us even though we were not born until after the death of your father. But now we seek peace and the place in the Fianna our father had before us.'

Fionn looked at them a long time. He very well knew that these young men were seeking a golden opportunity which they might not get again; they knew how unpleasant, how unsatisfactory and how lonely was the life of an outlaw, especially when it wasn't of their own choosing. They also knew, however, that all Fionn's vindictiveness was now directed away from themselves and their kind and towards the one who had done him the greatest injury of all, that to his pride – and in public. Fionn knew why Oscar and Oisin his own son and grandson, and their friends still felt friendly towards Diarmuid; quite apart from the obligations put on him by Graine, Fionn understood their unspoken sympathy for a young man in love with a young woman, and their resentment at an old man who coveted her; but their resentment was nothing compared to his own, first because they thought him old, and second because the insult had been public and was tacitly condoned in public.

Fionn realised that these young men now before him wouldn't have thought this out in such minute detail, but he guessed, and rightly, that they had a pretty good idea of the situation, borne of their burning desire to be outlaws no longer. They were here, he thought, to seize an opportunity, or to make one.

'I will grant your request,' he said at last, 'provided you pay me compensation for the death of my father.'

'We have no gold or silver or herds of cattle to give you Fionn,' they said.

'What more compensation do you want from them, Fionn,' asked Oisin, 'surely the death of their father is compensation enough?'

'It seems to me,' said Fionn drily, 'that if anyone killed me it would be easy enough to satisfy my son in the matter of compensation. But, as for me, none of those who fought at Castleknock, or their sons, will join the Fianna without paying whatever compensation I demand.'

'What compensation do you require, Fionn?' asked Aedh.

'The head of a warrior,' said Fionn, 'or a fistful of rowan berries.'

'Take my advice,' said Oisin to the men, 'and go back where you came from. The head he asks you for is that of Diarmuid O Duibhne, the most dangerous of all the Fianna, and the rowan berries are from the rowan tree guarded by Searbhan the giant Fomorian, and which is the more dangerous task of the two I could not tell you.'

But the two proud young chiefs would not listen to Oisin's advice saying that they would rather die in the attempt to fulfill Fionn's eric than go back to the outlaw life they had been living since childhood. So leaving their followers in the care of Oisin they set out on their quest and travelled north and west for several days until they picked up the track of Diarmuid and followed it to the hut he had built with the stout fence around it in Tirerragh. Diarmuid, who by now had become accustomed to alertness even when he slept, and in spite of the fact that the two young men were outlaws skilled in moving silently and unseen in bare and noisy places, heard them approach and snatching up his weapons he went out to confront them and ask them who they were.

Proudly they told him who they were and added: 'We have come here from Allen to get either the head of Diarmuid O Duibhne or a handful of berries from the rowan tree guarded by Searbhan as an eric to Fionn for our father having killed his father.'

Diarmuid looked at them in surprise for a moment at their candour, and then threw back his head and laughed.

'This is unpleasant news indeed,' he laughed, 'for me to hear, for I am Diarmuid O Duibhne and much as I admire you, friends, I am most unwilling to give you my head and you will find it no easy matter to take it. As for the berries, they are just as hard to get, for Searbhan is a formidable man who can only be killed with his own club.'

He looked at them then for a moment and went on

seriously.

'You are foolish men if you believe that Fionn will give you what you seek even if you are successful. He is making use of you for his own purpose and when that usefulness is over you'll find yourselves back where you were before, outlaws. Because that you will always be to Fionn. Now, which do you want to strive for first, me or the berries?'

'We will battle with you first,' they said. So Diarmuid opened the gate in the fence and made ready to fight them.

However, the two young men, who were extremely serious about their quest, proposed that they should discard their weapons and fight barehanded; if they were able to overcome Diarmuid, then they should take his head back with them to Fionn; if, on the other hand, Diarmuid defeated them, then their heads were his to dispose of as he saw fit. And seriously they began to circle the hero seeking the means of bringing him down. However, the fight was a short one. Diarmuid was not known as the most dangerous man in the Fianna without reason, nor had he taken part in many campaigns without learning much, and had they been ten times as many as they were, or twice that number, his task would have been little more difficult. Expertly and effortlessly he disposed of one and then the other. He did not kill them, for he had no bitterness towards them, but he knocked them senseless with subtle and calculated blows so that when they recovered consciousness they were bound hand and foot and Diarmuid was sitting on the ground in front of them, his legs crossed at the ankles, his back against a tree, his wife bending over a skillet in the background, gnawing on the leg of a pheasant and contemplating them.

'Well,' said Diarmuid, 'so you are awake at last. Did you sleep well?' he asked politely.

But they only glowered at him.

However, since they thought that he had only waited for them to recover that he could take their heads from them, this was understandable. But this was not Diarmuid's intention at all, even though he hadn't much of an idea what to do with them.

'I suppose you're hungry,' he said.

'What difference does that make,' said they, 'can't you take our heads and be done with it and stop playing with us.'

'Indeed, my friends,' said Diarmuid, 'and what would I do that for. Your heads are of much more use to you than they could ever be to me.'

'You mean you'll let us live,' they said.

'I do,' said Fionn.

'Well,' they said, 'aren't you the great man. Perhaps it's just as well we didn't go after the rowan berries first.'

And that's where something altogether unexpected and strange happened, for as they said this Graine, who was just coming up with something for them to eat, said:

'What rowan berries?'

Now Diarmuid knew his wife very well. He knew her proud, sometimes wilful, nature; the fact that she could be generous over big things – for she had never complained once about the life they were forced to lead – but sometimes rather selfish about small ones. In fact, she was a very womanly kind of woman. And because of this he had decided not to tell her about the rowan tree knowing that, whatever she might say, no woman could possibly resist the temptation held forth by a trio of berries which would prevent her from growing old; and how right he was! But witholding the information instead of doing good, now turned out to be infinitely worse. When Graine heard the story of the rowan berries from Aedh and Angus she turned to Dairmuid and said:

'And you knew about them all the time and never told me... oh!'

But her anger was over as quickly as it had come, and when the danger was pointed out to her it seemed to disappear altogether. But in its place grew and grew a tremedous desire to taste the rowan berries.

At first she tried to hide it, but, as it grew in her day by day Diarmuid realised what was wrong and became very troubled as, knowing his wife's mind when it was fixed on something, he feared that some harm might come to her if she could not get them.

Now the sons of Art Mac Morna had remained with them for all this time, bound lightly by the hands; for they were in no hurry to leave, and there was still hope that they could get the rowan berries, while, in addition, they were men of honour who owed their persons and their lives now to Diarmuid in any event.

So when they saw Diarmuid worried and troubled they asked him what was wrong and he told them about Graine's fixation with the rowan berries. 'Well,' they said, 'let us loose and we'll go with you to fight this Searbhan.'

Diarmuid laughed. 'I'm afraid the help I'd get from you two would be small enough once you saw him,' he said, 'but in any event, if I'm to fight him at all, I'd prefer to go alone.'

'No matter,' they said, 'our lives are forfeit to you now, so let us go with you, before we die, even if it is only to see you fight him.'

So Diarmuid agreed, and untied them, and the three of them went straightaway to the rowan tree. There they found the giant Fomorian, ugly as ever, asleep in the sun beneath the tree. Diarmuid gave him a heavy blow to wake him up. The Fomorian opened his bleary, red rimmed, eye and looked balefully up at Diarmuid.

'What ails you?' he said, 'there's been peace between us up to now, why do you come looking for trouble?'

'I'm not looking for any trouble,' said Diarmuid. 'But the Princess Graine, my wife, the daughter of King Cormac Mac Art, longs to taste one of these rowan berries and I am afraid that if she does not do so she will die. That is why I have come, and I beg you now to give me a few of the berries for her.'

But the ugly Fomorian, drawing himself up onto his feet so that he stood feet and inches above Diarmuid, looked down at him and said: 'I swear that if she, and all her line, were on the point of death this minute and one of my berries would save her, I wouldn't give it to her.'

Then Diarmuid replied, but there was a harder note in his voice this time: 'I don't want to take advantage of you and that's why I woke you up. I made my request openly wishing for peace between us. But now I want you to understand this, whether you agree or not, I will have some of those berries before I leave here.'

When the Fomorian heard Diarmuid say this, he lifted his great iron club and made three swings at Diarmuid which the latter had great difficulty in avoiding; indeed he didn't ward off the last of them which struck his shield and even though his shield was tough and his arm strong, it was numbed from wrist to shoulder. Then, watching the other closely and seeing that he expected to be attacked with sword and spear, Diarmuid suddenly sprang forward letting his weapons drop at the same instant and grabbed the huge man round the waist, taking him by surprise. With a quick twist, and a wrestling trick, he hurled the Fomorian over his shoulder so that he struck the earth with a mighty shock and then, picking up the great club, he gave him three blows dashing out his brains with the last one.

Diarmuid sat down beside the fallen Fomorian panting for breath, holding the bloody club in his hand. He dropped his head between his knees and only looked up when he heard the two young men who had watched the combat falling over each other beside him in praise of his achievement. With some annoyance he told them to keep quiet and if they wanted to be useful to take the body into the wood and bury it before Graine saw it and died of fright.

When they had done this Diarmuid asked them, for he was still tired after his battle with the Fomorian, to bring Graine to the tree and when they had done so he said:

'Now love, there are the rowan berries. Take what you want of them.'

But Graine was in that kind of mood that afflicts many women from time to time, and which had afflicted them and I suppose will always afflict them until the end of time; and the misfortune of it is this, that they have outrageous notions of what is an appropriate token of affection and esteem, perhaps, and set more store by that or some other triviality than they do by a thing that might rock the world. They will, for example, forgive a man easily for doing the wrong thing, but they will make a great noise about it if he does the right thing at what they would consider the wrong time. In these matters they are very particular. And so it was with Graine now. She was put out because Diarmuid didn't come running to her with his fists full of berries, and more put out when he just looked at her and said as if it was of no importance: 'Take what you want.'

So she looked anywhere but at him, and said: 'I will eat no berries except those that are plucked by my husband's hand.'

So Diarmuid, who was a very understanding man if he was

anything, stood up and plucked the berries for her and she ate until she was satisfied. Then he gave some to the two young men and said:

'Take these berries and go back to Fionn and tell him they are your eric fine. If you want to you can tell him too that it was you who killed Searbhan.'

'We will bring him one handful and no more,' they said, 'which is what he asked, and we grudge him even that.'

They thanked Diarmuid then, deeply and genuinely, before they left. And it was little enough for them to do since he had given them the berries to begin with, which they had not been able to get for themselves; and, although their lives were forfeit to him, he hadn't so much as mentioned the matter, but allowed them to go freely. So, bidding them farewell, the two knights went back to Allen.

When they had gone Diarmuid moved Graine and himself into the Searbhan's house among the branches of the rowan tree, where they lived on the rowan berries from that onwards; finding, as it happens, that while the lower berries were as honey and mead compared with any other food, they themselves were, as it were, bitter compared with the berries on the topmost branches.

When the two young knights reached Fionn's castle they gave him the berries, told him that Searbhan was dead, and asked that he fulfill his promise to accept them into the ranks of the Fianna.

Fionn took the berries in his hands and smelled them three times. 'They are indeed the rowan berries of Tireragh,' he said, 'but they have passed through the hands of Diarmuid O Duibhne, for I can smell his touch. And as sure as I do,' he went on, 'I am equally sure that it was he and not your-selves who slew the Searbhan.' And he looked piercingly at the two young men who hung their heads in acknowledge-ment. 'That being so,' said Fionn, 'you will not get from me either the peace you want or a place in the Fianna; for, apart from not getting the eric I put on you, you have made friends with my enemy.'

Now, when all this was done and the young knights banished again to the life of an outlaw, Fionn summoned his most trusted troops and set off for Tireragh where he hoped to catch up with Diarmuid finally. They followed Diarmuid's track to the foot of the tree and found the berries without anyone to guard them whatsoever.

Fionn looked round and grunted at what he saw. He made the troops pitch camp some distance away and then, since it was noon and the sun was high and hot and they were dusty and tired, said:

'We'll camp here under the tree, and this is where I'll stay myself.' Then he added as an afterthought, but one that he could not contain nevertheless, 'for I'm certain that Diarmuid is above among the branches of the tree.'

Oisin looked at him in amazement.

'You must be truly blinded by jealousy,' he said, 'if you think that Diarmuid is big enough fool to sit in a tree waiting for you when he knows you prize nothing more than his head.'

Fionn said nothing in reply to this, but he smiled the queer smile that had been growing in him lately and which sometimes worried those who knew him and loved him. However he called for a chessboard and men and himself and Oisin sat in the shade of the tree and began to play. Oscar and several more officers of the Fianna sat with Oisin while he played for there was none of them alone a match for Fionn and they were in the habit of playing him collectively. They played on for some time until there was one move which, if Oisin made it, would inevitably result in his winning the game. And Fionn said to him:

'One move, Oisin, and you can win the game, but I challenge you and all your helpers to make it.'

Now Diarmuid had been watching the game from the beginning and was following it closely; now he whispered to himself: 'If I was only below with you, Oisin, I could show you the move.'

Graine, sitting near him, felt her terror – which had mounted bit by bit since the Fianna arrived below them – grow great within her and she put a pleading hand on his arm. 'What does it matter if Oisin win or lose a game,' she whispered, 'when you might lose your head?'

But already he had plucked a berry from the tree and, flinging it down, struck the chessman that should be moved; Oisin made the move and, in time, won the game and the Fianna who had gathered round and were watching the contest raised a great shout. Whereupon Fionn leaned back in his chair, his two hands on the table before him, and looked at Oisin with a smile on his face.

'I'm not surprised,' he said, 'that you won the game Oisin, since you had the best help of Oscar, the skill of all these others and, above all, the prompting of Diarmuid O Duibhne from above.'

'Good Lord,' declared Oisin, 'has your jealousy no bottom to it that you think Diarmuid is up that tree waiting for you to kill him?'

And Fionn without changing his position, still looking at Oisin, just raised his voice and said:

'Which of us is telling the truth Diarmuid, Oisin or myself?'

'Yourself, of course, Fionn,' replied Diarmuid, 'for I'm here indeed in the tree.'

Then, looking up, Fionn saw them high above through an opening in the branches, and Graine, seeing that they were discovered, began to weep and tremble in anger. Diarmuid put his arm around her and began to kiss her and comfort her.

Fionn seeing this merely smiled, for his jealousy had now become hate. He ordered the Fianna to surround the tree in several ranks with their shields interlocked so that there could be no escape and he warned them on pain of death that they must not let Diarmuid pass. Having done this he offered large rewards; armour and arms, rank and position in the Fianna, to anyone who would climb the tree and either bring him Diarmuid's head or force him to come down.

Then a man from Waterford, called Garbha, whose father had been killed by Diarmuid's father, stood up and said that he would try; and began to climb the tree branch by branch. But when he reached a spot close to the hut, Diarmuid leaped at him from above and sent him crashing to the ground with a kick. Then one after another nine men who had real or fancied grievances against Diarmuid; or men who were ambitious or covetous tried to climb the tree after Diarmuid, but each of them was killed or sent hurtling to the ground to die there.

Meanwhile Angus Og had warning of the danger Diarmuid was in and he made his way through the throng of Fianna and fighting men as he had done before and to the hut in the tree and said that he would take Graine away to a place of safety. But she would not go until Diarmuid insisted and even then it was with much reluctance that she allowed Angus to wrap his cloak around her and take her in safety through the ranks of the Fianna below.

Then Diarmuid shouted from above down to Fionn: 'I'm coming down, Fionn. And be ready for you can be sure that I'll kill a lot before I'm killed myself, and I have no fear of death to stop me. There was never a time or a place that I wasn't prepared to die for the Fianna and for you in the past; well if I have to die now it'll be dearly bought by that same Fianna.'

'He's right, Fionn,' said Oscar, 'now is the time for you to forgive him before there's more harm done.'

'I will not,' said Fionn.

With that Oscar, Fionn's own grandson, leaped to his feet and cried: 'Shame on you. Then I, Oscar, now take the body and life of Diarmuid under the protection of my knighthood and valour and I pledge my word that, should the heavens themselves fall on me, or the earth open beneath my feet and swallow me, I will not let any man harm him here.'

'Come down, Diarmuid,' he cried, 'come down for you are no longer alone.'

Then Diarmuid, choosing the side where he had most concealment, leaped lightly to the ground beside Oscar and both champions faced the uneasy hosts of the Fianna. When Fionn saw Diarmuid his rage and hate boiled over and he seemed on the verge of apoplexy. But before he could summon his words Diarmuid and Oscar had passed through the silent Fianna, striking but a few blows here and there where the Clann Nephin tried to hinder them, like a pair of wolves through a flock of sheep and when Fionn would have rushed to follow them the Fianna linked their shields together and held him back. Then Deirdu, who had climbed the tree came down to tell Fionn that Graine was not there either and he knew that he had lost all. He had lost the king's daughter, the trust of his companions and his own faith in himself which was the root of much. All this Graine had taken from him when she passed him her goblet to drink at Tara so long before. And his heart was still unforgiving.

Meanwhile Diarmuid and Oscar had reached Brugh na Boinne where Angus had taken Graine and she died, as it were, a sweet death when she saw Diarmuid coming towards her bloody and torn from his encounter, but safe with her again.

CHAPTER FOUR

Diarmuid and Graine remained at Brugh na Boinne with Angus for some time and, during that period, the king, Cormac, succeeded in making peace between the embittered Fionn and Diarmuid whom he had outlawed. Fionn agreed to lift the ban of outlawry and also agreed that he would not, without Diarmuid's permission, hunt across the land to which Diarmuid was now entitled; that is the barony of Corcaguiny in Kerry, that of Ducarn near Douce Mountain in Leinster and that of Cos Corran which was given to Graine as a dowry; and it was here that they built their great house, Rath Graine; and it was here that Diarmuid prospered and grew rich in gold and silver and jewels; cattle and sheep and the produce of the soil.

Then, when they had lived there for several years, Graine – out of boredom or of pride or of whát, who knows, – persuaded Diarmuid to do two things that he didn't want to do: to give a great feast, and to invite the Fianna to it. They spent a year preparing the feast and it was celebrated for more than a full month.

One night as Diarmuid lay beside Graine he started up out of his sleep with such violence that she threw her arms around him in fear.

'What is it, little love,' she cried.

'A hound,' he said, 'I heard a hound baying.'

'But it is night,' she said, shivering in spite of herself.

'That is what I wonder at,' said Diarmuid, 'a hound that hunts at night.'

And she persuaded him to lie down again.

A second time he started up at the baying of a hound in the night, but Graine kept him back with the song of her love and her fear; which she had sung when they fled together from Tara.

> 'Sleep, my love, a little sleep
> There is no fear abroad to keep
> You from me, who owns my heart –
> Oh, my love; my Diarmuid.
>
> Sleep, as Fiach slept before
> When from Conall of Craevroe
> To the south he swiftly ran
> With the daughter of Morann.
>
> Sleep, as happy Fionncha slept
> When he northward Slaine swept
> To his bed in Assaroe
> Where cautious Failbhe dared not go
>
> Sleep as Ann slept in the west
> When softly to her lover's breast
> By torchlight from her father's farms
> She fled to Duach's loving arms.
>
> Sleep, as proudly in the east
> Dedaid slept when flight had ceased
> With Coinenn, for whom his life he'd sell,
> In spite of bloody, warring Deill.
>
> Who'd separate my love and I
> Must separate the sun and sky;
> Must part my body and my soul,
> Oh soldier from the bright lake shore.'

And he slept; but before the dawn broke on the east the baying in the night awoke him again from his slumber, and this time he made a song for her to show how distressed he was and to signify the urgency that was within him.

'That roaring stag with stamping feet
That roves the night, he cannot sleep;
No thought of sleep within him stirs
Who tramples down the homes of birds.

The lively linnet does not rest
Leaping through tree-tangled tresses;
Making music in the night,
With hurried thrushes taking flight.

The slender duck is restless too
Swimming on from place to place;
She will not sleep or cease for rest
Drawing danger from her nest.

Tonight the curlew does not sleep
His music's high above the deep
Rage that through this midnight screams;
He will not sleep between the streams.'

Then Diarmuid left the bed and stood in the middle of the floor as if listening to something, but Graine could not hear a thing. 'There it is again,' he would say, and she would shiver, as he stood there with his head to one side. Below in the yard his own hound Mac An Cuill ran about whimpering and trying to hide itself, shivering, beneath a cart.

'I'll go and find that hound I heard baying in the night,' said Diarmuid.

'Oh, don't go,' she said, 'don't go where I cannot see you to-day.'

But Diarmuid would not listen to her protests.

'In that case,' she said, 'take the Moralltach with you and the Gae Dearg, so that you will be prepared for any danger.'

But he laughed at her.

'What danger could there be in such a small matter, and anyway they are too heavy. I'll take Beagalltach and the Gae-Buidhe instead.'

'Can we not talk to-day of the feast we will give to the King?' asked Graine, 'and you can hunt to-morrow?'

'That is a good idea,' said Diarmuid, 'but to-day is a good day for hunting and to-morrow will not be a bad day to talk about the giving of a feast.'

And so he went off to the mountain and there, in the dawn, he found Fionn standing alone. Diarmuid gave him no greeting, but asked him where the hunt was and Fionn told him that some of the Fianna had left Rath Graine during the night with the dogs and one of the hounds came across the spoor of a wild boar and both men and dogs followed it.

Even as Fionn spoke there was a faint baying below them. And Fionn went on:

'I tried my best to stop them for this is the boar of Ben-bulben who has been chased often, and as often killed men and dogs before him. He has already killed several of the Fianna this morning and, as he is tearing his way towards us I think we would be wise to move to a safer spot.'

But Diarmuid would not leave.

'Leave the hill and the boar to the hunters, O'Duibhne,' said Fionn, 'I do not want you here.'

'Why should I leave the hill,' said Diarmuid, 'I'm not afraid of a boar.'

'Then you should be,' said Fionn, 'for you are under *geasa* never to hunt a boar.'

Then Fionn told Diarmuid the story of what had happened so many years before in the palace of Angus at Brugh na Boinne and of the curse that the steward had put in Diarmuid that night. When he had finished Diarmuid looked at the other man, standing there in the dawnlight with a single hound, Bran, beside him.

'What you say may be true, if it is I don't remember it,' said Diarmuid, 'but in any case it would be cowardly of me to leave the hill before I had sight of the boar. I'll stay here, but would you leave Bran with me?'

Fionn didn't answer him, but, with Bran by his side, went down the hillside. Then Diarmuid stood with his own hound, Mac An Cuill, shivering beside him as the great boar came charging at him through the undergrowth. Suddenly it burst through the bushes, huge and black, its little red eyes glaring hatred in the dawn, its great tusks curving backward from black, foam flecked lips; the ground trembling under the razor-sharp feet of the heavy shouldered monster as it bore down on Diarmuid. Diarmuid unslipped Mac An Cuill, but the hound turned and ran in terror.

Then Diarmuid remembered what Graine had said to him about taking his heavy weapons and muttered: 'Bad luck to him who doesn't heed the advice of a good wife.'

Nevertheless he slipped his finger into the silken loop of his smaller spear, the Gae-Buidhe, and hurled it with all his might at the oncoming monster. The spear struck the boar between the little glaring eyes, but not a bristle, not a piece of skin, was cut, not a gash nor a scratch made in the terrible beast.

When he saw this Diarmuid guessed it was his end, but, drawing the Beagalltach in one, swift movement, and with a great battle-roar, he hurled himself at the oncoming monster and made a tremendous stroke at the broad neck with the full weight of his body behind it. But to no purpose for the sword splintered in pieces off the thick hide, while not a bristle of the boar was hurt, leaving only the heavy hilt in Diarmuid's hand. And even as he made the stroke the boar pitched him so that he fell across the humped back, and hurled him to the ground. Then the furious boar crashed through the brush, and turned back again, rushing at Diarmuid and gored and pitched and ripped him with his tusks until the hero was a mass of bleeding wounds both outside and in. Turning, the beast was about to renew the attack when, summoning his last strength, Diarmuid flung the hilt of his sword at him, driving it through the skull to the brain, so that the brute fell down dead on the spot.

Now as Diarmuid lay dying from his wounds, Fionn and the Fianna arrived and saw him beside the body of the boar.

'Oh my grief,' cried Oisin rushing to his side, 'to see you here like this, torn by a pig.'

'And mine,' said Fionn, 'that the women of Ireland are not here to see your beauty and grace torn away by a pig.'

'Fionn,' said Diarmuid, 'you speak with your lips and not your heart. You have the power to heal me if you will.'

'I am no leech,' said Fionn indignantly.

'It was given to you to heal a wounded man with a draught of water carried by your hands,' said Diarmuid.

'That is true,' said Oisin.

'And why should I do this for you, above all men?' asked Fionn.

'I'll only remind you,' said Diarmuid, 'of when you were

surrounded in a thatched house by your enemies who threw firebrands on the roof and how I and a few of my men rushed out and quenched the flames and made a circuit of the place slaughtering your enemies before us so that you were safe. Had I asked you for a drink that night you would gladly have given it to me.'

'Unfaithfulness changes everything,' said Fionn, 'and the world knows how unfaithful you were to me when you carried Graine from me in the presence of the men of Ireland.'

'Do not blame me for keeping the geasa under which I was pledged,' said Diarmuid, 'but remember how when you were treacherously invited to a feast by the King of Wales and captured I came to save you when he would have handed you over to the Romans; and how I kept the Welsh and the Romans at bay with my men until you were rescued, and all the other things I have done for you since I first joined the Fianna.'

Then Oisin, Fionn's son, said: 'I cannot allow you, Fionn, to withhold this drink from Diarmuid, and I say now that if any other prince in the world should think of doing Diarmuid such treachery there would leave this hill only whichever of us had the strongest hand.' He said this his eyes flashing with angry fire, looking directly at his father. 'Do what I say and bring the water to Diarmuid.'

'I don't know where there is a well on this mountain,' said Fionn sullenly.

'There,' said Oisin pointing angrily, 'is one nine steps away from you.'

Slowly Fionn went over, the contempt of the Fianna lying heavily on his shoulder, and filled his hands with water. But he had not gone more than four paces when his jealousy overcame him again and he let the water slip allowing it to spill through his fingers saying that he was not able to carry water so far.

Diarmuid groaned when he saw this, and said: 'You let it slip yourself, Fionn, for I saw you. Hurry now, for I'm close to death.'

Fionn looked around guiltily and when he saw the stern faces of the others he returned to the spring and again took a handful of water; but again when he turned towards Diarmuid and thought of Graine he let it slip through his fingers.

When the others, Oisin and Oscar and Diarmuid's other friends saw this they lifted their spears and turned them against Fionn, and Oisin cried out:

'We will not allow this treachery.'

Then Fionn went a third time, and this time he carried the water to where Diarmuid lay. But even as the general of the Fianna stood above him with the life-giving handful of water, Diarmuid's spirit passed from him with a groan and he died.

There was silence, a stillness on the hilltop then. All the men of the Fianna, the officers and Fionn, stood as in a tableau still and immobile until Diarmuid's hound, Mac An Cuill, came through them and raised a mournful howl above the body of his master. Then Oscar looked across at Fionn and said:

'I wish it was you instead of Diarmuid that lay there, Fionn.'

But Fionn walked away from him, turning his back, and stood lonely beside the spring where he had gathered the water to bring to Diarmuid. And Oisin, his son and Oscar's father looked at his lonely back and said:

'No draught of water can heal you Fionn, or make you any different from what we now know you to be; an old, embittered and cunning man, caring for nothing but yourself – who was the emblem of us all.'

Caoilte looked a long time at Fionn, and then said: 'The strength of the Fianna will wither away because of this, Fionn. We can never hold you in the same esteem again, but as you have planted the acorn, let you bend the oak yourself.'

Then Oisin and Oscar and Caoilte and Diorraing covered Diarmuid with their cloaks and mounted guard over him. Then Mac An Cuill came to Fionn, who put him on a leash to lead him back to Rath Graine, but Bran, his own hound, refused to come to him; and sadness covered the whole mountainside. So Fionn, leading the hound, and followed by the men of the Fianna except for the four who stood guard above Diarmuid, left the mountainside and made his way towards Rath Graine.

Graine herself was standing on the ramparts of her castle when she saw the chiefs of the Fianna coming towards her, Fionn leading Mac An Cuill, and a sudden fear that had been haunting her all that day went through her. 'If Diarmuid were alive,' she whispered in terror, 'it is not Fionn who would be leading his hound.'

And when Fionn came and told her that Diarmuid was dead she fainted and did not recover there upon the ramparts for a long time. But when she did and when she knew that what she had been told was true she raised a cry of grief that echoed and rechoed in the glens and wilderness around, startling the birds in their nests and the wild beasts of the field and forest in their lairs. And then she ordered that five hundred of her people should go and recover the body of her husband with all the pomp and ceremony that he demanded, and so they went. But when they got to the mountaintop there they saw the hosts of the de Danaan with Angus Og at their head and their shields reversed as a sign of peace. And both armies, having viewed the dead hero, raised three mighty shouts of sorrow, so loud and great, that they were heard across the margin of the world and over the five provinces of Ireland.

Then Angus asked them what they had come for and they said to carry the body of Diarmuid back to Rath Graine, but he would not let them saying that Diarmuid was his foster-son and he would take him with him to Brugh na Boinne.

'There I will preserve him,' he said, 'for although I cannot breathe life back into my foster-son again, I can breathe a spirit into him so that for a little while each day he can talk to me.'

Then he placed the body on a golden bier and, with Diarmuid's weapons raised before it, the people of the de Danaan, carried it to Brugh na Boinne.

When Graine's people returned and told her what had happened she was griefstricken and angry at first, but later she accepted the idea and lived alone, and in peace with herself for some time. Meanwhile Fionn had returned to Allen with the Fianna, but his days there were gloomy and unhappy for the trust that had existed between himself and the Fianna was there no longer. But after a year of living like this, one day and without telling anyone where he was going, Fionn left Allen and made his way to Rath Graine. When he got there Graine received him coldly at first and asked him what he wanted from her.

'I come in peace,' he said, 'and to offer a place in the

Fianna to your sons when they have grown.'

At first Graine would not listen to him and turned away in disdain. But after some persuasion, when he pointed out the benefits it would be to her sons to get high places in the Fianna, her interest quickened.

'But who would guarantee that,' she asked.

'Yourself, Graine,' he answered. 'For there is no man fitter for you to marry now than myself, and no woman fitter to be the wife of Fionn Mac Cumhal than yourself.'

Then Graine turned from him in disgust and hatred. But the more she did, the more he persevered and impressed her at last with his sincerity and, odd though it may seem, his apparent humility. And at length she agreed.

And at last, after he had been away for some time, the men of the Fianna saw them both coming towards Allen across the plain and when they saw who was with Fionn they raised three great shouts of derision and mockery, and Graine hung her head in shame.

But Fionn took her hand and led her into the great hall of his castle at Allen. But there was never the same spirit abroad in the Fianna after that, even though Fionn and Graine lived together with mutual support until one of them died.

But that night at a banquet that Fionn gave, Oisin could not restrain the hurt that stirred in all of them, and his bitterness against the fickle woman, and he said aloud where it could be heard: 'I trust my father will keep her fast from this time onward.'

And so ends the story of Diarmuid and Graine.

The Sickbed of Cuchulain[1]

Just as the story of the Children of Lir belongs to a time that
is in the remote ages of man's memory, when gods and men
walked the earth together and there was not that much distinction between the two, and that of Diarmuid and Graine
belongs to a time that is so close to our own that it can be
measured in terms of time and of men such as are about us
to-day, this story falls between the two. Conor Mac Nessa
ruled Ulster with the aid and assistance of his noble lords, the
Red Branch Knights of whom the most famous were Naoise
and his brothers, Ainle and Ardan, the Sons of Usna; Fergus
Mac Ri, true king of Ulster; Connall Cearnach, terrible in
battle, and the youthful but mighty Cuchulain himself.

Now every year at Samhain, that is at the end of summer
and at the beginning of autumn, the people held a feast for
seven days; three days before summer ended, on Samhain itself, and for three days at the beginning of autumn. And on this
occasion the festival was being held on Magh Muirtheimne,
the plain of Muirtheimne, between the River Boyne and Car-
lingford Lough which was the home and inheritance of
Cuchulain... and it is said that the place got its name from the
words *muir,* the sea or a tide, and *teimen,* secret or concealment because at one time it was covered with the water of the
sea until the Dagda himself caused the water to recede. But
it is far more likely that it was a name given simply to the
hinterland of that beautiful, deep and concealed lough itself.

Anyway, it was here that the festival was held at the time
of which I write, and gay, splendid and joyful it was; with a
great market and fair lasting for the week, a continuous feast
of dancing, music, song and merry-making of all kinds, together with joustings and armed competitions among the
knights.

Now, one evening, while Cuchulain sat in the shade of a
tree – for it was still hot – playing chess, a great flock of

1. See introductory note.

white birds came and landed on the waters of the lough close by. They were strange and unusual birds such as had never been seen there before and the women who were there with Emer, Cuchulain's wife, at the lakeside talking to one another, began to say how much they would like to have these birds, until one of them, in the way that women do these things, said with an eye on Emer, 'If my husband was here he would catch some of those birds for me.' 'Or mine,' said another, and then another until they were all giggling among themselves and looking at Emer and nudging each other for Cuchulain was the only one near them at the time, apart from the knight he was playing who was an old man. Then Emer, proud within herself, but not for the sake of pride, beckoned Laeg, Cuchulain's charioteer, and said to him that the women wanted the birds and asked him to tell Cuchulain. Aloud she said, for she was a very true woman too, 'If anyone is to have these birds, then it is I who should have them first.'

Laeg went to Cuchulain and said: 'The women of Ulster would be well pleased if you brought them those birds there.' Cuchulain didn't answer him, but went on playing chess.

Then Laeg tried again: 'The women would like you to catch some of those birds on the lough for them.'

This time Cuchulain looked up in anger. 'Have the women of Ulster nothing better for me to do than to go chasing birds for their amusement?'

'It isn't right,' said Laeg, 'for you to speak against them like that. For it is on your account, and for love of you, that they have assumed one of their three blemishes.'

Now this was the truth; for the three blemishes of the high-born women of Ulster were lameness, stammering and bad eyesight; the first was assumed by the women who were in love with Connall Cearnach, because of his limp, the second was assumed by those women who were in love with Cuscraidh Mian, the king's son, because of his difficulties in speech, and the third was assumed by those – more than either of the other two put together – who were in love with Cuchulain because in his battle rage a form of blindness, akin to that of a berserk, overcame him and distorted his features.

So, with bad grace, he growled at Laeg; 'Bring me my chariot – a fine thing it is for me to be doing, catching little birds for women!'

Then, angrily, he drove his chariot along the water's edge and hurled his curved, Egyptian sword so that it flew like a boomerang and returned to him; and the birds fell, their feet and wings flapping the water so that it was easy for them to be gathered up by Laeg. Then Cuchulain drove to where the women were and, with his anger still in him, he threw the birds at their feet and turned his chariot away without a word. He drove to where Emer was, but he had none of the birds left for her; and he did this deliberately because of his anger, but already was regretting it.

'You are angry with me,' he said.

'No,' she replied, 'why should I be angry with you? You gave the birds to those women, and it is to me as if it was I who had given them. You did right, for there isn't one of them who does not love you; and none in whom you have not an interest. But as for me, no one has any share in me except yourself alone.'

And she said this with a certain bitterness, for there was truth and love in it at the same time, and they do not always make a sweet mixture.

Cuchulain was sorry then for his anger and his infidelity to Emer with the other women, and he said: 'Whenever in the future strange birds come to the plain of Muirtheimne, the two most beautiful will be yours...'

Hardly had he spoken when they saw, sailing out of the distance and bearing down on them across the lake, two glorious birds, more beautiful than any of the others, and linked together by a chain of red gold. As they came, slowly and majestically, they made soft, sweet music that lulled all who heard it to sleep except those close to Cuchulain.

'There are your birds,' he said to Emer.

But she was afraid. 'There is something strange about those birds,' she cried, 'leave them fly on in peace.'

'Are you serious?' said Cuchulain in derision, 'put a stone in my sling, Laeg.'

Laeg did so and Cuchulain fired, but for the first time since he had taken arms the cast missed.

'Well,' he said, 'that is a strange thing that never happened to me before.' And he fired again, and again he missed. And a third time he tried, and missed also. Then, in his anger, he threw his spear at them with true aim, but the spear suddenly deflected and passed through the pin feathers of one bird only.

Then, in his rage and frustration, Cuchulain took out after the birds and followed them until they rounded an outcrop of rock in the lake and disappeared. When he reached it they had vanished. And though he gazed out across the lake, and up into the clouds of heaven, there was no sight of them and he could not tell where they had gone to. Then, suddenly, for no explicable reason, he felt unutterably weary and listless and he stretched out on the sward and leaning his back against a pillar of stone, he slept. Then, as he slept, in a dream which was more real than any dream he had known before that, two women came towards him. One of them wore a green cloak and the other a purple one folded in five folds. The woman in the green mantle carried a little sally rod in her hand and, laughing all the time, she came towards Cuchulain in his dream and began to strike him gently with it. Then the other did the same, laughing too, as if they played a game with him, and for a long time they did this, each of them in turn, and it seemed to him that whenever he was struck with one of the rods, the strength in his body departed from that place.

He lay like that until the men of Ulster found him and they were worried and upset because of the way he lay so still and entranced. And a group of them decided to waken him, but Fergus stopped them saying that Cuchulain saw a vision. Shortly after that Cuchulain came out of his sleep and they asked him what had happened. But the weakness was still on Cuchulain and it was all he could do to ask them to carry him to the Speckled Hall of the Red Branch Knights. The Speckled Hall was one of three halls set apart from the king's palace at Emhain Macha. In the Speckled Hall they hung their weapons and stored their trophies and it was because of the glitter made by the reflected light of the sun off the gold and the bronze and the iron that that hall was called the Speckled Hall and it was there that they carried Cuchulain and laid him on a bed with his own weapons above his head. And he lay there like that for a full year with his friends and comrades keeping guard and watch over him. And at the end of that time, when Samhain had come round again, a stranger came and visited the Speckled Hall. Silently and unannounced he came and stood among them. He looked at Cuchulain and said:

'If the man lying there were in his health, he would protect all Ulster. But, even though he is sick, he is still my protector, more so even than if he had his health, for it is to see him I came and I am sure that none here would injure me while he is unfit to protect me with his sword.'

'Welcome then,' said the men of the Red Branch Knights.

Then the stranger sang this song to Cuchulain, which none of those there could follow except the sick hero:

> 'Cuchulain, there's no need to lie
> In sickness as you do.
> Aedh Abhra's daughters here will fly
> And bring the cure to you.
>
> Liban, who reigns as Leabhra's queen
> On Crooagh's plain has cried:
> 'Lovely Fand must sleep or die
> At Cuchulain's side.'
>
> Cried Fand: 'How well that day will shine
> When Cuchulain comes;
> To him I'll offer all that's mine
> And gold in mighty sums.
>
> 'If here with me Cuchulain lay
> in sunshine or in dew;
> I would his dreams, by night and day,
> Have made them all come true.
>
> 'To where Muirtheimne's plain is spread
> Liban will go from me;
> At Samhain stand beside his bed
> And cure his malady.'

And who might you be anyway?' demanded the Red Branch Knights when the stranger had finished this song.

'I am Angus,' he said, 'son of Aedh Abhra and brother of Fand.' And then he left as he had come, without any seeing where or how. Then his friends crowded round Cuchulain and asked him what it was all about, but he was nearly as mystified as they, except that he understood the words of Angus's song. And this was one of the first questions they asked him and when he told them that he did understand, they pressed him to tell them, which he did.

Then, when he told them, he asked King Conor what he should do, and the king replied:

'Cuchulain, for a whole year you have lain in sickness unable to speak or move for want of strength. Now, at Samhain again, you have made something of a recovery. And my advice to you, in the light of what Angus has said, is to go again to that pillar stone and see if Liban has a message for you.'

So Cuchulain was carried in a great cart to where the pillar was against which the sickness descended on him a year before, and when he arrived there he saw the woman in the green mantle there before him.

'It is good that you are here,' she said to him.

'Little good it has done me,' said Cuchulain, 'since I came last year. What brought you then?'

'It was to do you no injury that we came,' she said, 'but to seek your friendship. I've come from Fand, the daughter of Aedh Abhra and my own sister. Her husband, Manannan Mac Lir has released her, and she has turned her love on you and will not live without you. My own name is Liban and I am the wife of Leabhra the Swordsman, king of Moy Mell. He has asked me to seek your help against Senach the Spectre and Eochaid Euil and Eoghan of the Stream, who have declared war on him with all their unearthly hosts.'

Now Cuchulain knew of Fand, who was beautiful beyond the beauty of all women of the world, with an unearthly loveliness. Because her face and person were perfect and flawless she was named Fand, which means 'tear', for there was nothing else so wonderful and flawless with which she could be compared. And she lived with her sister and her husband, Leabhra, in their country of Moy Mell.

Nevertheless Cuchulain replied: 'I am in no fit state to go to war. But let Laeg go with you, and he can bring me back a report of what he sees.'

'That weakness will not last you long,' said Liban. 'And

115

soon you will have your strength back again, greater than before. Meanwhile, let Laeg come with me if he will.'

Then, taking Laeg under her protection, she brought him to the plain of Moy Mell by secret and enchanted ways. During the journey she looked at the charioteer and teased him: 'You would never make this journey, Laeg, if you were not under a woman's protection.'

Laeg didn't think the joke amusing, and replied with dignity: ' 'Tis not a thing I have been accustomed to doing, putting myself under a woman's protection.'

Then, without thinking, Liban half aloud murmured the thought in her mind: 'It is a great pity that it is not Cuchulain who is under that protection.'

'Indeed,' replied Laeg angrily, 'it would be a great deal better for me if it was.'

Eventually they reached the shores of a great expanse of water and a bronze boat, small and light, bobbed about waiting for them. They entered it and it took them to an island off the shore and so to the door of Leabhra's palace. Before the palace were armed men and Liban spoke to one of them and asked him where Leabhra was, for she knew the king would be gathering his troops for the impending battle.

And, indeed, that is exactly what the officer said he was doing; but was able to add that he was at that very moment on his way back to the palace. Even as he spoke there was the distant rattle and thunder of a war chariot coming at a gallop and in an instant it swept up to the palace gate and was hauled to a stop by the straight, towering, stern-faced warrior who held the reins with stiff-muscled arms.

Lightly tossing the reins to one of the officers nearby, he jumped down without looking to see if he caught them, and strode towards Liban and Laeg. At his side hung the huge and terrible two handed sword from which he took his nom-de-guerre. He was frowning now, and worried looking, as Liban went forward to greet him.

Glancing doubtfully at Laeg, Leabhra — for that is who it was — asked: 'Has Cuchulain come?'

'No,' she replied, 'but Laeg is here, and he will surely come to-morrow.'

Leabhra made no reply to this, but his disappointment rose and added to the frown on his face.

She laid her hand on his arm. 'Don't worry,' she said, 'Cuchulain will be here. You are the strongest and the wisest; your law is just and so are your battles, you cannot fail.'

But Leabhra turned away from her a trifle impatiently in his worry and said: 'Proud words, Liban, are out of place this day. My enemies have immense armies ranged against me and it isn't boasting of my ability I feel like, but lamenting my weakness.'

'Look,' she said, to turn his mind away from such thoughts, 'there is Laeg, and Cuchulain will be here to-morrow.'

Then Leabhra remembering his duties, greeted Laeg: 'Welcome,' he said, 'for the sake of him you come from and of her you have come to see.'

And at that Liban said to Laeg: 'Will you go now and see Fand?'

Laeg agreed, having paid his respects to the king, and Liban brought him through the palace to Fand's quarters. And as they passed through the palace he looked out of a high casement across the plain and there, in the dim distance, he saw the armies of Senach the Spectre, Eochaid Euil and Eoghan of the Stream assembling, silently and in masses, filling the distant plain. More and more of them he saw, advancing and filling the distance; their spears glinting in the sun and their banners waving against the sky; but, although there were countless numbers of them, there was no sound of armour and horses; no clashing of weapons and rasping of metal as they came onward noiselessly; the only sound to be heard was a low, soft wailing like that of wind in the trees of the forest.

'To-morrow,' said Leabhra, 'there will be battle, and we cannot stand before that host unless Cuchulain comes.'

'He will surely do that,' said Laeg.

Then, having greeted Fand, Laeg returned to Cuchulain and told him all that he had seen and heard. Immediately Cuchulain's strength began to return to him and his mind was strengthened in him for the news that Laeg brought.[1]

* * * * *

Then Cuchulain said to Laeg: 'Go to Dun Dealgan (which

1. See introductory note.

was where he had his castle) and see Emer for me. She has been waiting now for a year. Tell her what has happened, that I had a fairy sickness, but that I am getting my strength back now. Ask her to come to me.'

Laeg did as Cuchulain asked him and went to Dun Dealgan where he found Emer in great grief not knowing why she had not heard from her husband... although in those days, it seems, such was the enlightenment of the people that for the most part wives were not expected to be curious about their husband's whereabouts especially when they were on some knightly errand or other; and the probability is that because they didn't worry, there was nothing for them to worry about.

At all events it was not like that with Emer, and possibly she had more justification for her attitude than most women of her time, for already half the noblewomen of Ulster were openly in love with her husband and even in those liberal times when a man – or a woman – could openly acknowledge a deep and pure love without fear of social ostracism if it did not conform to certain rules; even in those times the wife of a great and distinguished man might well be jealous in spite of her love for him and his for her.

When Laeg told her what had happened Cuchulain, she was bitter and angry. 'Shame on you,' she cried, 'and shame on the men of Ulster. If it was one of them – aye, or yourself, indeed, master Laeg – who had been bewitched with a sleeping sickness, my Cuchulain would not have rested until he had found some cure. But not one of them would think it worth their while to do the same for him. If it was Fergus, his foster-father, Cuchulain would have gone through the earth for him; or Connall Cearnach, he'd have scoured the earth, or Laoghaire, or any of the others, he wouldn't have stopped night or day until he had the power to heal him. But they do nothing for him when he's struck down, except stand around his bed, you tell me, looking sorrowful and waiting for him to cure himself. It would make you sick. Friends indeed!'

Then, having spent her anger on Laeg, she instructed him to take her to the Speckled Hall at Emhain Macha as quickly as possible that she might be with Cuchulain when he recovered.

And when she arrived and saw him, still weak, but conscious, her tenderness and pity and love turned in her bosom; but her distress and the memory of the past year made her angry with him all over again that he should languish like this under an enchantment. And, in her typical womanly jealousy, she upbraided him unjustly for something he wasn't guilty of at all (at that time at any event), but loving him the greater all the while she did so.

'Shame on you,' she cried, 'to lie there like a schoolboy for a woman's love.'

And so she taunted him and provoked him and gradually his spirit returned, though whether from her anger of from the lifting of the enchantment by Liban is not known; at all events he improved and greeted Emer.

Then again he went to the place where he had seen Liban the year before, and she was there again before him. He spoke to her and greeted her, and she welcomed him and pressed him to come with her to Moy Mell to assist Leabhra in the battle. But Cuchulain hung back. Then, said Liban, 'Fand waits for you with the world of her love to offer you.'

But Cuchulain still resisted. 'I will not go at a woman's call,' he said. 'Well then,' said Liban, 'let Laeg go and confirm what I have told you.'

'Very well,' said Cuchulain, 'let him go with you.' So Laeg went with Liban across the Plain of Speech and past the Tree of Triumphs, over the festal plain of Emhain and the festal plain of Fidga until they reached the palace of Leabhra where Fand was. And she asked: 'How is it that Cuchulain did not come? To which Laeg replied: 'He didn't care to come at the summons of a woman; moreover,' he staid, 'he wanted to know if it was indeed from you that the message came and wanted to know all about this place.'

'It was from me,' said Fand, 'and now return and bring Cuchulain quickly for the battle is to-morrow.' Then Laeg returned to where he had left Cuchulain, who asked him:

'How does it look to you, Laeg?'

'Good,' replied Laeg, 'there is happiness and a battle before you,' and he told him what he had seen.

'While I was on this great journey
A wonderous township I did see –
Though all I saw seemed normal there –
Where I found Leabhra of the Long Hair.

There he sat upon a hill
His armoured troops surrounding him;
His glittering hair, with colour dappled,
Was tethered by a golden apple.

He looked at me before he spoke
From his five-folded purple cloak;
'Come, Laeg, and we will go within
And meet my regent, Failbhe Finn.'

Into the palace me he brings
Where three hundred serve the kings;
So mighty is their palace, great,
That all reside within its gate.

The couches are scarlet and golden and white
Jewels for candles disseminate light,
The couches are bounded about a great hall
And there's room, and to spare, there for then

Westward of the palace gate
The dying sun's rays illuminate
A stable full of dappled greys
Another too, as full of bays.

While eastward from the palace grow
Three crystal redwoods in a row
Whose branches ring with singing birds,
The sweetest sounds I ever heard.

And in the palace court I sought
That tree of tinkling silver wrought
Which will accompany anyone
And glitters gaily in the sun.

Sixty trees whose branches meet
Drop fruit in plenty at their feet;
Enough to feed three hundred each
With fruits more pleasant than the peach.

Within the palace there's a maid,
More lovely than I ever prayed
To see in Erin: With golden hair,
She's beautiful and skilled and fair.

A woman all mankind might seek.
A wonder 'tis to hear her speak.
The hearts of all she talks will break
With love and longing for her sake.

She looked at me awhile and said:
'Who is this youth, where was he bred?
If you are from Muirtheimne too
Come here and let me look at you.'

Slowly, for I moved in fear,
To her side I ventured near
Conscious of the honour done.
'Where,' she asked, 'is Dechtire's son?'

Long before you should have gone
When those that lived there urged you on,
That, like me, you might have seen
What dreams are real, what might have been.

Were all of Ireland mine to give
I'd give it all, if I could live,
Aye, and Bregia's kingdom too,
Whence I returned in search of you.'

'Then you think I should go,' asked Cuchulain.

'I think you'd be a fool not to,' said Laeg, 'everything there is wonderful and there is danger too, for they are threatened with war immediately.'

Then Cuchulain and Laeg returned with Liban and journeyed over the Plain of Speech, beyond the Tree of Triumphs, across the festal plain of Emhain and that of Fidga until they came to where Leabhra and his chiefs and officers waited for them. And a great and tremendous welcome was given to Cuchulain. But he did not wish to waste time in ceremonies for he knew, from what he had heard, that the battle was imminent and, though he acknowledged his welcome graciously, he did it briefly, and then, turning to Leabhra, he said:

'Let us go and take a look at the enemy.'

So Leabhra mounted into Cuchulain's chariot with the champion from Ireland and together with a few picked men, they set forth to observe the enemy dispositions. When they reached the great plain not far from Leabhra's palace it was covered as far as the eye could see with the black tents of Senach the Spectre, and from the pole before each tent hung a black pennant. Among the tents they could discern black-clad warriors moving or riding blood red horses with fiery manes. Over the lot hung a mist, low over the tent ridges, so that the full extent of the host was obscured, and from out of the mist came the low moaning sound of the demon host.

When Cuchulain saw this frightening assembly his spirits revived within him and his blood began to run hotly and boil for action. 'Come on,' he said to Leabhra, 'let us circle them and see how many they are.'

But, although he drove his chariot in ever widening circles, the black-clad enemy sprang up before him wherever he turned to go, behind them as innumerable as the blades of corn in a field, or the stars in an autumn night; grim and gaunt they faced him on their blood-red steeds. It seemed to Cuchulain that the smell of blood was already in the air, but instead of daunting him it gave him all the more courage and anger.

Turning to Leabhra and his officers again he said: 'Leave me now, and take your troops with you, for this battle I must fight alone.'

Reluctantly the king did as Cuchulain ordered him to, because he said he would not fight at all unless he did it his own way. And when they saw him left alone to face the demon hordes, two ravens, the spirits of the Morrigu who were allied with Senach, fluttered and cawed about the hosts trying to tell them that it was Cuchulain that stood before them. But they laughed at the birds' antics, saying: 'It must surely be the madman from Ireland who is there alone.' And they chased the ravens away so that there was no resting place for them in the plain with the moaning laughter of Senach's troops.

All that night Cuchulain stood with his hand upon his

spear watching the enemy. Then, as dawn broke, his battle-rage came upon him and his whole aspect changed and altered terribly. It is said of him that one of his eyes retreated into his head so that it could hardly be seen, and that the other extended forth so that it was as big as a fist; that a column of red blood sprang from the top of his head and that his body became so hot that it burned those who came within feet of it; and with all that his rage and fury and strength were that of a hundred men. Such was the change that came over the noble youth in his fury.

Just as dawn spilled gently over the hills to the east, one of the enemy chieftains, Eochaid Euil, left his tent to bathe himself in a nearby stream; he removed his tunic and, as he did so, Cuchulain hurled his spear and transfixed him where he knelt. Then, without pause, and in the wild ferocious rage of his battle fury, he leaped among them and killed them right and left. Thirty-three men he killed outright before Senach the Spectre attacked him himself and tried to rally his men; but the battle did not last for Cuchulain slew him with a terrible blow of his sword and, as he did so, the army of Leabhra fell upon the demon hosts and drove them in confusion from the field. But still Cuchulain would not stop and he pursued the fleeing soldiers cutting them down as he did so, so that dead and dying lay behind him like a bloody path across the plain wherever he went. Then Leabhra tried to stop the fight for he was sick of the slaughter, and called on Cuchulain to stop. But to no avail. For his battle-fury was still on the hero, and Laeg turned to Leabhra and said:

'Go easy, Leabhra, that he might not turn his fury on ourselves for he has not fought himself out,' and Laeg was frightened for he knew well the terrible wrath in Cuchulain.

'Then what will we do?' asked Leabhra.

'Go and get three huge vats of water,' said Laeg, 'and bring them here. I will persuade him to go into them. The first vat into which he goes will boil over; no one will be able to bear the heat of the second vat after he comes out of it and after he has been in the third vat it will have but a moderate heat, and that is how we will bring him to his senses again.'

So this was done. Laeg persuaded Cuchulain, with no little danger to himself from the hero's bloody and dripping sword, to enter three vats. And when he emerged from the third he was himself again, hardly more than a boy. And they took him and bathed him, and scented him and gave him fine clothes to wear and after that brought him to Fand who was waiting for him.

When he came before her, refreshed and scented; his hair bound and oiled and swept into a golden ball on his head; his bearing proud, yet youthful too, she thought that she had never seen anyone half so wonderful before and her heart went out to him. And he, in his turn, when he saw Fand, knew that he had never in his life seen a woman so beautiful as Fand. She asked him to sit beside her, and her musicians and maidens sang a song of praise for Cuchulain that she had made for him. And after that she asked him to tell her of the battle, which he did, but with a modesty that belied his feats. And then, with darkness drawing in and the jewelled lamps throwing out their rays, she dismissed her women and her musicians and Cuchulain slept with the lady.

He stayed with her for a month. But at the end of that time he felt a desire to return to Ireland and, though he loved her, he told Fand this. But she was upset and terrified that she would lose him and tried to keep him with her, but to no purpose, for he had his mind made up to return to Ulster and the Red Branch Knights.

'I am a hound of war,' he said to Fand, 'not a little dog to play about his mistress's feet; I must go and stand before the enemy and battle for my country and my king.'

When Fand saw that he could not be persuaded to stay with her, she was sad, but bade him a gentle and loving farewell; all those who had befriended him were sad at his going and Leabhra, in particular, came and thanked him for his help against the demon hosts. Having thanked Cuchulain Leabhra asked Liban to take him back again to Ireland. Before he went Fand looked at him with great love and tenderness and said:

'Tell me where and when I may meet you again and I will be there.' And they agreed that their meeting place would be the Strand of the Yew-Tree's Head.

And so Cuchulain returned to Ireland and he and Laeg were greeted warmly by all their friends in the Red Branch and by Emer; and he told them all about what had happened except that to Emer he said nothing about Fand. But she got to learn about her and about their meeting place at the Strand of the Yew-Tree's Head.

The more she learned the more her hatred and jealousy grew and then, one day when she knew that Cuchulain had gone to keep his rendezvous with Fand, she took fifty of her women with her and arming each of them with a strong, sharp dagger, she set out to kill Fand. Silently they crept to the place where Cuchulain and Fand sat in the shade of a yew tree. Cuchulain and Laeg were playing chess and were unaware of what was going on. But Fand, whose senses were keener than those of either, heard the women approaching and then saw them and immediately realised their intention.

'Look Laeg,' she cried.

'What is it,' he asked sharply, jerking up his head.

'Behind you,' said Fand, 'Emer and her women coming through the undergrowth. Cuchulain, they are armed and against me I don't doubt.'

Cuchulain turned and saw the women led by Emer and saw that Fand was right into the bargain.

'Don't be afraid,' he said to Fand helping her to her feet. 'Get into my chariot and I will protect you. Emer will not harm you as long as I am here.'

Then, turning to Emer, he said:

'Put down your knife, Emer. I cannot fight you back and you would not kill me in spite of your rage. It would be ironic if I were to be killed by a woman when I've been so victorious on the battlefield.'

'Then tell me,' she cried in anguish, 'why have you shamed me and dishonoured me before the women of Ulster and all Ireland? What have I done that you have turned away from me and loved another woman, and a fairy woman at that?'

'Emer,' said Cuchulain, 'it may be true that I have broken my vow to you; but where is the gravity of the fault? How could I not love Fand too? She is fairer than the fair, more beautiful than the beautiful; intelligent and talented and a fit wife for any king and moreover has a mind that is as keen and able as the best. There is nothing under heaven that a wife would do for her dear husband that Fand has not done for me. Therefore do not lay too much blame on us. And as for yourself, where else would you find anyone who has loved you as I have, or who shows you so much reflected honour?'

Emer laughed scornfully at him. 'In what way is she better than I am,' she asked. 'Men are all alike. What's red seems fair and what's white seems new. Men worship what they can't have, and what they have seems nothing. We lived happily together, Cuchulain, and would again if you only loved me.'

'Indeed,' said Cuchulain, 'I do love you, and always will as long as I live.'

'Then,' said Fand unhappily, 'I must go.'

'No indeed,' cried Emer, 'it is better that I should be the one who is deserted.'

'No,' said Fand. 'It is I who must go.'

A terrible sadness and loneliness seized Fand then, and her soul was great within her, for it was a terrible shame for her to be deserted and returned to her home; moreover the mighty love that she had for Cuchulain was tumultuous in her. Then she made this lament:

> 'My heart is turning in me,
> Yet I must go my way;
> My love remains behind me –
> If I could only stay.
>
> Nothing could be sweeter
> Than your loving hand,
> I would choose it rather
> Than my native land.
>
> Emer, gentle lady,
> I set your husband free;
> Although my arms release him
> Longing stirs in me.'

Then she lifted up her lovely face and Emer saw teardrops, so well fitting her own name, welling in her eyes.

But now a strange thing took place. Manannan, who had been Fand's husband and who had released her, learned that Fand was in danger from the women of Ulster and that she was likely to be left by Cuchulain whom she loved. Thereupon he came from the east to help her. Manannan was old, so old

126

that no one knew his age except himself. He was kingly and majestic, but feared too by men, for his moods were terrible and variable, though he could smile benignly when it suited him. But now, when he saw Fand's great distress, he came swiftly to help her, invisible to men, but not to her. And as he passed her she felt his presence and looked up as he passed. But for a moment she did not know him, for he had shed his years and the man she saw was young and strong, with a noble gentleness upon his face.

Then she cried to herself, looking into her heart, and said: 'Oh God, here is Manannan. Once he was dearer to me than the world we shared, yet to-day, though his voice is music to my ears, no love and exultation fills my heart, for the pathway of love may be bent astray and its knowledge depart. Oh Manannan,' she cried, 'when we lived together in the past our life was an unending dream. It seemed as if nothing could divide our love. I know that no one save myself can see you and that you can understand all; but that is no help to me now. Being a woman I am helpless now that the man I love has left my side.' Then, turning to Cuchulain, she said: 'Cuchulain...' but could say no more for her grief overcame her.

Then Manannan said to her: 'Fand, what will you do? Will you come with me or stay here until Cuchulain comes to you?'

Then in anguish Fand looked at him, her love turning like a live thing inside in her bosom, and she said: 'Dear Lord, Manannan, I do not know. Either of you is a greater man than any woman could wish for, and neither of you is better than the other. Yet he has betrayed me and, besides that he has a wife to love him already while you have none. Therefore, Manannan, I will go with you.'

Then Manannan stretched out his arms to her and she went to him. And Cuchulain seeing her go, for he could not see Manannan, cried out: 'What is happening, Laeg? Where is Fand going?'

And Laeg, who had the ability to see the great one, said: 'She is going back to Manannan since you do not love her above all else.'

Then Cuchulain gave three great cries of grief and rushed about in despair, so wildly and madly that he did not stop until he came to the desert of Luachra. And he lived there for a long time, eating no meat and drinking no wine and sleeping by the highway that goes to Tara of the kings. Then Emer went to Tara and spoke to the King about Cuchulain and what had happened to him in his grief for Fand. And the king sent out his physicians and doctors to cure him and bring him back to health and to Emhain Macha. But Cuchulain had so lost his wits that when he saw them he ran from them at first and then tried to kill them, until at length he fell in a fit from weakness and begged a drink from them. This they gave him, but with it they mixed a drug which dulled his memory and sent him into a deep sleep. When he woke from it the memory of his passion was gone, though there lingered a deep sorrow in him. And the physicians gave a similar drug to Emer to help her to forget her jealousy, and with her it was more successful and her natural joyousness returned. But she was troubled to see Cuchulain so sad.

Then Manannan, who learned of the trouble between Emer and Cuchulain, shook his cloak between Cuchulain and the beautiful Fand so that from both of them the memory passed away as though it had been a dream, and they thought of each other no more.

And that is the story of the Sickbed of Cuchulain.

First published in the Netherlands
Made and printed in Holland by
N.V. Drukkerij Bosch